HOW TO TEACH YOUR OLD DOG NEW TRICKS

Ted Baer

With Photographs by the Author

BARRON'S

New York • London • Toronto • Sydney

Photo Credits
The photos on pages 8 and 9 are used through the courtesy of *Mark Sennet/VISAGES*.

Important Note
Training may require some physical exertion on the part of the trainer and dog. Do not take any health risks! The training in this book is not recommended for aggressive dogs. If your dog shows signs of aggression, seek the help of a professional trainer.

All inquiries should be addressed to:
Barron's Educational Series, Inc.
250 Wireless Boulevard
Hauppauge, NY 11788

International Standard Book No. 8-8120-4544-0

Library of Congress Catalog Card No. 90-21742

Library of Congress Cataloging-in-Publication Data

Baer, Ted.
   How to teach your old dog new tricks / Ted Baer.
     p. cm.
   ISBN 0-8120-4544-0
   1. Dogs—Training. I. Title.
  SF431.B35 1991   90-21742
  636.7'088'7—dc20   CIP

PRINTED IN HONG KONG
1234 9927 987654321

**To my wife Lynnette,
Both irresistible and
irreplaceable!**

Acknowledgments

Many people deserve thanks for their help with the general appearance of this book. Each chapter had a different, enthusiastic volunteer. Their ages ranged from thirteen to seventy-one. Twenty-five different dogs participated, representing nineteen different pure breed and five mixed breeds of known ancestry. Most of the dogs have never had any formal obedience training. They all did a wonderful job, and I am deeply indebted to both human and canine volunteers. Thanks to the following for making this book special:

Mary Babin
Denny Bouchie
Marc Bouchie
Margo Breen
Melanie Brewer
Jessica Clements
Ila Dombowsky
Jeanne Fowle

Liz Johnson
Nancy Johnson
Andrew Kort
Carolyn Lamar
Lois Mayerchak
Pat Maynard
Dave Peterson
Aimee Powell
Jill Ross

Mary Schmitt
Bob Smedley
Scott Smith
Alan Stewart
Betsy Wahlberg
Richard Webb
Mary Weight
Noelle Williams

Note: The pronouns used in the captions are based upon the gender of the canine model shown in the photo.

Contents

Introduction:
Start Anywhere!

I'm sure everyone has met a few dogs that they thought were brilliant—veritable four-legged geniuses who amazed simple mortals by performing a trick, maybe even two. The clever owner of the dog never jumped in and said, "Without me this dog would have trouble finding its tail!" He loved being the proud owner of the smartest dog on the block!

People want to believe that they've met a wonder-dog, not just a dog that has been cleverly trained. One question I'm frequently asked about my

star pupil, Tundra, is whether I accompany her to the studios when she's filming. I have to bite my tongue to keep from saying that she has her own bus pass! The common belief is that Tundra was born a genius. She's hardly the smartest dog that ever existed, but she just might be the one that's acquired the greatest amount of skills. What seems to be human-like intelligence was actually taught!

Success in dog training comes from effective communication. You undoubtedly know that effective communication is hard enough with people, let alone with dogs! But bear in mind that Fido just wants to please you. He'll be happy to accommodate your requests if he understands what it is you want him to do. Being aware of whether your dog is getting your message or not will help you to understand your dog better. It will also allow you to be more effective in trying to communicate with him. If he isn't getting the message, ask yourself why. What's confusing him? You will discover it is almost always something *you* are doing wrong! If you're interested in bridging this communication gap with your dog, my book *Communicating with Your Dog* (see page 142) covers this in depth.

Most pet owners want to teach

erence directs you to the pages where you will find a full explanation and supporting photographs. At the end of each trick, a list of other tricks that share similar training is provided. This will prove to be a real timesaver. Odds are that you won't have to buy anything to teach these tricks, since only commonly found items are used for props.

The following general suggestions will help you throughout the book. It is most important that you try to stick to the exact words and hand signals I recommend. Your dog will learn 39 new word commands if you teach him every trick in this book. Consistency in using the same words, the same logical word order, and the same method of speaking is necessary for clear communication. The

their dog a few tricks. Until now the process required too much ingenuity and a lot of dog-training knowledge. Inevitably, this led to major frustration. This book reveals the small, simple steps you should follow in teaching each trick. Alternative approaches to teaching particular tricks will also be offered. A trick that appears complex and impossible to teach even to the smartest dog is successful for that reason alone! All the seemingly difficult tricks in this book can easily be taught to any dog.

Start anywhere in this book. You'll find that each chapter is a complete unit. When a particular trick makes use of a basic behavior component—like *sit* or *stand*—a cross ref-

hand signals used are each unique from the dog's point of view. You have to trust me on my selections; space limitations preclude an in-depth explanation of why certain words or hand signals are used.

Gear the length of your training sessions to your dog's attention span. Allow your dog to succeed throughout each session and be sure to end it on a high note. At the end of each session, make a habit of playing with your dog. He'll look forward to the play period and, in doing so, maintain his enthusiasm during the training session. If your dog falters on a particular step of a trick you are teaching, you are probably proceeding too fast. Go back to where you can end the training on a positive note and move on to something else. In your next session, back up a little in your training and rebuild your dog's confidence. It may take you 20 or more five-minute training sessions to teach a trick. But for less than two hours of training, your dog will look as if he's ready to apply for a scholarship to your local university!

To avoid monotony for yourself and your dog, work on the different elements of a particular trick or on several different tricks during the same training session. Try to make a little progress with each element and move on to the next. Wrap up the training session at the slightest sign that your dog is tiring. You'll see terrific progress if you follow these suggestions!

Throughout your training sessions keep a constant flow of positive feedback going to your dog. Like humans, dogs that are complimented for a job well done, rather than condemned for a few mistakes along the way, will progress faster and more happily. Try to remember this throughout the book, since there won't be room to remind you on every page!

There are several good ways of praising and encouraging your dog for correct behavior. My two favorite rewards are a good scratch and the use of the word *good.* An intermixing of play and work is fun for both of you, too. At the end of a training session a chew toy makes a good reward. For general dog training, I suggest that you get to know what pleases your dog, then try to vary the rewards among those favorites. In trick training, I lean toward using food rewards most of the time and occasionally mixing in others. I find this method the most effective and time efficient.

Using food rewards will be a terrific motivator. The smallest of treats works the best to keep your dog motivated and happy. I usually use a one-cup measuring scoop of dry dog food. A kernel of dry food is small enough to be eaten quickly so that you can get right back to the training. Your dog will consider it a welcome reward. Chapter 8 covers the training involved in teaching your dog to catch kernels of dog food. Place this training at the top of your list! Tossing the reward is very convenient for you, as it will keep you from having to travel to your dog each time a reward is in order. It's a real timesaver. In addition, it's good dog training. Whatever the reward, it should be given immediately so that the dog associates the reward with the particular action that pleased you.

To maintain consistency and keep from confusing the dog, it is best to have only one trick trainer in the household. However, once a trick is completely mastered, it can be demonstrated by anyone. You should require the person to know the commands and hand signals, and to attain a certain level of performance from your dog before rewarding him. You don't want your training reversed.

All training of new material should be taught in a place that is free from distractions. This gives your dog the best opportunity to learn. After a trick is mastered, practice it in different locations and with different distractions. You want your dog to perform regardless of life's noises, unfamiliar odors, and the presence of other animals or young children.

If you are this far along in the introduction, chances are you've given this book a good home and you'll be giving performances with your dog in the future. As you pick the tricks you'd like to work on, remember to keep variety in mind. Don't pick three retrieving tricks to do back-to-back in your performance. Instead, alternate them with nonretrieving tricks. Your audience will never notice any similarities and it will make for a better show. Feel free to use any of my humor from the book during a performance. Chances are you'll come up with other humorous lines for your situation. You want to loosen up your audience. They'll enjoy the performance more. Also, try to reduce possible distractions before a performance. Often a radio can be turned off or a cat can be placed in a back bedroom.

In just a month of working with this book you'll find that you will have acquired a lot of dog-training knowledge. You'll also have a good idea of how to break down any trick into small, simple parts so that you can teach it. Once this occurs, you might consider putting your own imagination to work on possible tricks that are not covered in this book. I think you'll have a lot of fun with it.

I really enjoy teaching and playing with my dogs. I receive more positive feedback from my dogs and from the people who see them than from any other thing I do. I'm sure you'll find teaching the tricks in this book an enjoyable way to further the education of your dog, while leaving him panting for more. But the best part, by far, is that these tricks allow your dog to unleash his animal magnetism on everyone he meets!

Brewster, a four-year-old basset/shepard, finds it's not a problem to retrieve a tissue.

Chapter 1

Not to Be Sneezed At

Retrieving a tissue upon hearing you sneeze.

This very simple trick is a real crowd pleaser. Upon hearing you sneeze, your dog will retrieve a tissue and bring it to you. People will look at your dog in disbelief. The trick is a success because you don't use an expected command to set your dog in motion. It appears to be a voluntary reaction to your involuntary action!

Start by locating the perfect place to demonstrate the trick. Your living room or family room will probably be ideal. Imagine the crowd. Will everybody have a good view? The trick will lose a good deal of its impact if you

have to repeat it because some people couldn't see. Now, consider your options for placing the tissue box. If

Of the two tissue boxes shown, use the boutique style (shown on the far left). It always has a protruding tissue.

possible, position it in the same room in a spot that looks very natural. But try to anticipate possible problems. Will your dog be able to reach the spot if the room is crowded? Might damage occur because of your dog's paws or weight?

The only exception to placing the box in the same room would be if there is a powder room located just off the area you've picked. In this case, although your audience might not actually see the dog place his paws on the vanity, they probably will *hear* it. The subsequent shock of seeing him return with a tissue will be great! However, you must make your audience aware that you are doing a trick with your dog. This can be accomplished by first doing another stunning trick to get everybody's attention and then exaggerating the sneeze to indicate that you are up to something.

There are two basic styles of facial tissue boxes—the more traditional, rectangular box and the taller, almost square, "boutique" box. Use the boutique box because it always has a protruding tissue. That makes it easier for your dog to grab it.

You will need to prepare the tissue box before the demonstration. Tape the box down so that it won't move. Use small loops of masking tape (sticky side out) and stick them to the bottom of the box so that the tape doesn't show. Nobody needs to know you've taped it down. Be forewarned that masking tape can damage certain items. In most cases it won't, however, unless you leave it on for a long time.

Use a tissue box that has been partially emptied. It is hard to pull a tissue out when the box is tightly packed. Prepare the particular tissue that your dog will grab by pulling one out and stuffing it back in. The object is to make the tissue as easy to grab as possible and to leave the box appearing normal after the trick is done. To get the box to look normal after your dog pulls out the tissue, slightly fold the second tissue into the first when you tuck it back into the box. This will allow the second tissue to pop up, and will prevent your dog from grabbing them both at the same time. You'll be a pro at preparing the box after just a few training sessions!

There are four behavior components in this trick:

1. Placing the front paws up on something.
2. Jumping up on a chair or couch.
3. Retrieving a tissue.
4. Delivering a tissue.

The first two components are optional. They will give you flexibility on where to place the tissue box. Although you could locate the tissue box on a coffee table well within your dog's reach, the trick is more impressive when you add a little more complexity. The components should be taught independently. Once you've completed a short training lesson on one, however, you can start the training of the next in the same session.

1. Placing the front paws up on something.

To teach your dog to place his front paws up on an item, grab some tasty treats and position yourself next to the item. Say your dog's name followed by the command *"Come, paws up."* Hold a treat in your fingers and tempt your dog into reaching up. Immediately give him the treat. Try to get him to reach a little farther each time. Remember to reward your dog for even minor progress. Over several training sessions (and 20 to 100 treats later!) your dog will be standing on his fully extended hind legs with his paws on the item.

If you are having trouble with your dog putting that first paw up, give him an uplifting experience. Physically, but gently, assist him. With both of you facing the item, straddle your dog with your legs. Place one of your hands under his chest and the other under his front leg. Lift him gently, touch the paw to the desired destination, and immediately reward him. Repeat this several times to get him used to it and then return to coaxing him to do it on his own.

Once your dog is placing his front paws up on the item consistently each time, teach him the command "Go, paws up." Move away from the item a few feet and try it. You and your dog should be standing and facing it. Say his name followed by the command "Go, paws up" as you swing your arm toward it. In subsequent training sessions, gradually increase the distance you send him.

2. Jumping up on a chair or couch.

This is an optional step that you only need to teach your dog if he is unable to reach the tissue box when on his hind legs. Depending on the situation, a chair or couch might work well. Make sure that it feels stable and solid. If your dog jumps on a chair with casters, for instance, it is apt to roll away from him. If it does, he may be afraid to jump up on any chair in the future. To simplify the explanation of the training, I'll be referring only to training your dog to jump up on a chair. The general training can easily be applied to the use of a couch.

The word *up* will be used for positioning your dog above the floor, the ground, or a particular level. It directs him to attain something at a higher level than he is at present.

Start the training by having your dog sit facing a chair approximately three feet away. Have your treats ready, and stand behind the chair so that the chair is between you and your dog. Say your dog's name followed by the command *"Come, up"* while patting the cushion of the chair. When he jumps up, quickly reward him with a treat. This should be easy for most dogs. Initially, they will respond more to the hand signal of patting the cushion than to the verbal command. If your dog has difficulty, it is probably because of previous training to keep him off the furniture. Try to entice him with food. Physically help him up into the chair, if necessary, while showering praise on him. Be patient, and keep everything positive. He'll catch on quickly!

As soon as your dog is responding to the *come, up* command, start increasing his distance away from the chair before you give the command. Then proceed, but do not pat the chair anymore. Back up a few feet in a line with your dog and the chair, and try it again. Over several training

This is the proper position for gently helping your dog put that first paw up on something.

by the command *"Go, up."* Take a step forward, pat the chair, and reward him when he gets up on the chair. Increase the distance slowly and continue traveling quickly to the chair with him each time. Gradually decrease the patting of the chair until it is unnecessary. Next, instead of you traveling to the chair, allow your hand to swing out toward the chair as you give the command. If your dog is slow to respond, quickly run toward the chair, directing him. Soon he'll understand!

3. Retrieving a tissue.

The preliminary training for the retrieve is covered in Chapter 18, "Retrieving an item," page 106. Once the retrieve is mastered when using your dog's favorite toy, practice the retrieve with a variety of easily held items. Just walk around your house handing him things and, of course,

sessions, make progress in each of these areas. Remember to reward him each time he succeeds. Take it step by step. If he gets confused, repeat the previous steps.

Once your dog has learned the *come, up,* it's time to teach him the *go, up* command. Position yourself and your dog a few feet in front of the chair. Say your dog's name followed

Teaching your dog to jump up on a chair.
Left: Say your dog's name followed by the command "Come, up" while patting the cushion of the chair.
Right: Quickly praise and reward.

You will find this hand signal useful in teaching the go, up *command.*

rewarding him for his compliance. Now that he's skilled in this area, it is time to have him retrieve a tissue. Review the training steps, using a tissue as the object of your desire. Additionally, you need to preface the use of the verbal command *get* with an exaggerated sneeze. Give a theatrical sneeze, then give the appropriate verbal command. It won't take long for your dog to start reacting to your sneeze, allowing you to drop the verbal command completely. Be sure to take his training one small step at a time.

4. Delivering a tissue.

The preliminary training for delivering an item is covered in Chapter 18, pages 108–110. Once the delivery is mastered using your dog's favorite toy, practice having your dog deliver a tissue. He should adapt well to the changing of the delivered item.

Final Thoughts

As soon as your dog's training has progressed well with each of the components of the trick, combine the training as a unit. Also, if you plan on taking this trick on the road, practice it with the tissue box in all different locations. (It's up to you to teach him to say, "God bless you!")

When you have taught this trick, you will have a head start in teaching the tricks found in Chapters 3, 7, 12, 16, and 18.

Chapter 2

Done on the Spot
Chasing a flashlight beam.

In this trick your dog will chase the beam from a flashlight until he is able to "catch" it. Much like the flashlight, your audience will beam from the dog's antics as he tries to get it. It's a simple trick if he is a good retriever already. If he is not, the training for this trick will strengthen his skills. Either way he is bound to hit the spot!

There are three behavior components in this trick:

1. The *stand* position.
2. Chasing a favorite toy.
3. Chasing a flashlight beam.

The *stand* is one of the major body positions a dog can assume. It will be easier for your dog to learn the trick if he remains in this position. After you've completed a short training lesson on the *stand,* you can proceed to the second component, but be aware that he needs to remain in the standing position.

You should wait to teach the third component until your dog is thoroughly proficient at chasing a favorite toy.

1. The *stand* position.

Please refer to Chapter 22, pages 124–125, for the training of this behavior component.

2. Chasing a favorite toy.

The object of getting your dog to chase his favorite toy is to give him knowledge and skill that can be transferred later to chasing the flashlight beam. To do this, a simple prop needs to be made. Take one end of a two-foot cord and tape it to the end of a broom handle. Next, attach the other end to your dog's favorite toy. Again, use tape if necessary. This prop has many similarities to the flashlight beam he'll chase later. Like the beam, the prop you made is under your control, is chased by your dog at floor level, and can be safely used without the possibility of incurring an accidental nip on your hand from overenthusiasm.

To teach your dog to chase his favorite toy, use the prop to tease him into chasing it. It is best to use a carpeted area or go outdoors in the grass. This will provide him with the traction he needs and prevent injury. As you do this, it is not necessary for you to move much with the broom. Hold your ground, but move the broom around to tempt him into chasing his toy. Pretend you're fishing and keep the bait just a foot away from his nose. Tell him *"Get it"* and when he grabs it, praise him by saying, *"Good."* This feedback word is a very effective training aid. Then, exchange the toy for a tasty treat. Do not play tug-of-war with the toy, or you may have trouble getting him to release it to you later. If you have trouble with him releasing the toy, usually a strong *"No!"* and a quick exchange of the toy for a tasty treat will work. Drop the toy to the ground again, and repeat this exercise until he's skilled at catching up with it. Don't be too good at keeping the toy away from him. Allow him to succeed by making your initial moves easy; as he starts to improve his skill, increase the difficulty gradually.

Once your dog has mastered the chase with his favorite toy, it is time to change to an object that is more like the beam of a flashlight. Cut an eight-inch diameter circle of cardboard and attach it to the end of the cord. A white piece of cardboard is ideal because of its contrast with the floor. Try to minimize the tumbling effect of the cardboard by letting it slide along the floor. You'll find that carpet has an advantage over grass in doing this. Again, make a game out of it and tease him into chasing the circle for a treat. Because the cardboard is flat, he will begin to pounce on it and capture it with his paws instead of his mouth. Practice this several sessions until he is proficient at chasing and capturing the circle. Then, cut the diameter of the circle down to five inches and try it again. Later, cut the circle down to two inches and practice. This gets him used to chasing any size circle.

If you are having trouble getting him to chase the circle at all, back up in the training and use his favorite toy to practice again. Next, try some of his other toys and several new items. Spend time getting him used to chasing anything you put on the cord. Before trying the cardboard again, rub some roast beef on it to make it more interesting. His instinct to chase things is on your side and he should be having a lot of fun!

3. Chasing a flashlight beam.

It is best to train your dog to chase a flashlight beam in the same area you've already been working. Initially, do your training at night so that your dog can't miss seeing the beam of light. Leave a dim light on in another room to provide you with a trace of illumination. Start the training with lights on in the area and get him

warmed up by having him chase the cardboard. Reward him. Now, turn off all but the dim light and introduce the flashlight beam by shining it on the floor in front of him. As with the previous training, command him to *"Get it."* When he tries to grab it, immediately praise him and reward him with a treat. Make sure you turn off the flashlight immediately as he makes his first attempt at it. This will provide him with additional positive feedback. Don't be too picky at first. You only need him to move toward the beam at this stage. He'll pick up his enthusiasm quickly with practice. Just as you previously did when you used his favorite toy, tease him into chasing the beam over several training ses-

sions. Make sure you turn off the flashlight and reward him quickly each time he pounces on the beam. Once he is doing well in the darkened area, gradually increase the light in the room during your training sessions until he can perform in daylight.

If you are having trouble getting your dog to chase the flashlight beam, you probably proceeded too quickly. Either back up in the training or try kneeling down on the floor and holding a treat in the beam of light as you move it. With repetition, you can make gradual progress toward your goal. Once the dog is responding, discontinue holding the treat in the beam and use only your empty fin-

In teaching your dog to chase his favorite toy, tease him into following it.

gers, instead. Then reward him with a treat using the other hand. The next step is to simply point to the beam from an inch away. Gradually increase the distance between your pointed finger and the beam of light. This method is bound to put him on the spot! Your enthusiasm is the biggest key to this trick, so keep it flowing.

Final Thoughts

You wouldn't have purchased this book unless you wanted your dog in the spotlight. With this trick, fresh batteries are all you will need to accomplish that!

When you have taught this trick, you will have a head start in teaching the tricks found in Chapters 10, 13, 17, 20, 22, 24, and 25.

Your dog will have fun chasing the cardboard if you reward him with a treat each time he captures it.

Chapter 3

Double Exposure
Flipping a light switch.

In this trick your dog will head over to the room's light switch, place her front paws on the wall, and turn the switch on. Like the bulb, your dog will shine! After the crowd's enlightenment, your dog will return to turn the switch off. The end of the trick involves a momentary pause to receive the admiration of all. Try to look modest!

Initially, you'll do all your training using one particular light switch. Once your dog has mastered the trick, you can familiarize her with every switch in the house. The trick is very practical and cost effective. You don't need technology to have remote-controlled lights in your house. When you get in bed at night and forget to turn off the light, you have a trusty friend that will enjoy doing it for you!

Start by locating the most suitable light switch for the training. For demonstration purposes, it should be a single switch in a common area. The switch should work in the usual way: when pushed up it's on, when pushed down it's off. Make sure that the area below the switch is easily accessible to your dog. Imagine a crowd in the room. Does everyone have a good view? The trick will lose

a lot of its impact if you have to repeat it because some people couldn't see. The switch should control a major light in the room so that people can tell when your dog has completed her assignment. Before a demonstration, turn off or dim some of the other lights in the room for a better effect.

Once you've found the most suitable light switch for your purpose, make sure the switch cover is free of cracks for safety sake. You will want to protect the wall throughout the training process. This can be accomplished easily by mounting a piece of thick cardboard over the work area. A piece about two feet by two feet will work well for medium to large dogs. You will need either a larger piece or an additional piece that extends lower when training a small dog. After the initial training, the small dog will be working off a chair and the lower portion of cardboard can be removed. Cut a hole slightly larger than the switch cover near the top of the cardboard. Try to avoid damaging the wall when attaching the cardboard. Depending on the wall, thumbtacks, masking tape, or rubber cement might be used.

Train at dusk or night so that your dog receives visual feedback in addition to your verbal praise and food treat. At night, you'll have to leave a dim light burning in the room so that you and your dog can see the switch.

There are four behavior components in this trick:

1. Placing the front paws up on the wall.
2. Jumping up on a chair.
3. Turning the switch on.
4. Turning the switch off.

You should teach your dog the components one at a time, waiting to proceed to the next step until the previous one is mastered. The second component is included in the event that your dog can't reach the light switch with her muzzle when standing on her hind legs. Depending on your dog's height, you may be able to skip this step.

1. Placing the front paws up on the wall.

To teach your dog to place her front paws up on the wall, grab some tasty treats and position yourself next to the wall switch. Say your dog's name followed by the command *"Come, paws up."* Hold a treat in your fingers and tempt your dog into reaching up the wall. Reward her attempt with the treat. Try to get her to reach a little farther each time. Remember to reward your dog for even minor progress. Over several training sessions (and 20 to 100 treats later!) your dog will be standing on her hind legs with her paws fully extended up the wall.

If you are having trouble with your dog's putting that first paw up on the wall, you may have to physically, but gently, assist her. With both of you facing the wall, straddle your dog with your legs. Place one of your hands under your dog's chest and the other on her paw. Lift slightly, touch her paws to the wall, and immediately reward. Make her reach a little bit more each time and reward.

Once your dog is placing her front paws up on the wall consistently each time, teach her the command *go, paws up.* Move a few steps away from the wall and try it. You and your dog should be standing and facing the wall with the light switch. Say her name followed by the command *"Go, paws up"* as you swing your arm toward the wall. In subsequent training sessions, gradually increase the distance you send her.

2. Jumping up on a chair.

This is an optional step that you need to teach your dog if she is unable to reach the wall switch when on her hind legs. Depending on her height, you'll need to find a suitable chair, hassock, bar stool, or combination of furniture that allows her to reach the switch. Whatever you se-

Ch. Shannon C.D., a five-year-old flat-coated retriever, is bound to turn on her audience with this trick!

lect, make sure that it feels stable and solid. If your dog jumps on a chair with casters, for instance, it is apt to roll away from her. If it does, she may be afraid to jump up on any chair in the future. To simplify the explanation of the training, I'll be referring only to training your dog to jump up on a chair. The general training can easily be applied to jumping onto other furniture, into the car, onto a grooming table, etc.

The word *up* will be used for positioning your dog above the floor, the ground, or a particular level. It directs her to attain something at a higher level than she is at present.

Start the training by having your dog *sit* facing a chair approximately three feet away. Have your treats ready, and stand behind the chair so that the chair is between you and your dog. Say your dog's name followed by the command *"Come, up"* while patting the cushion of the chair. When she jumps up, quickly reward her with a treat. This should be easy for most dogs. Initially, they will respond more to the hand signal of patting the cushion than to the verbal command. If your dog has difficulty, it is probably because of previous training to keep her off the furniture. Try to entice her with food. Physically help her up into the chair, if necessary, while showering praise on her. Be patient, and keep everything positive and happy. She'll catch on.

As soon as your dog is responding to the *come, up* command, start increasing her distance away from the chair before you give the command. Then proceed, but do not pat the chair anymore. Back up a few feet in a line with your dog and the chair, and try it again. Over several training sessions, make progress in each of these areas. Remember to reward her each time she succeeds. Take it step by step. If she gets confused, repeat the previous steps.

Once your dog has learned the *come, up,* it's time to teach her the *go, up* command. Position yourself and your dog a few feet in front of the chair. Say her name followed by the command *"Go, up."* Take a step forward, pat the chair, and reward her when she gets up on the chair. Increase the distance slowly and continue traveling quickly to the chair with her each time. Gradually decrease the patting of the chair until it is unnecessary. Next, instead of traveling to the chair, allow your hand to swing out toward the chair as you

give the command. If your dog is slow to respond, quickly run toward the chair, directing her. She'll soon understand!

Once your dog has mastered jumping up on the chair, have her jump up on the chair and place her front paws on the wall. Review the previous training for placing front paws on the wall, if necessary, until both steps are combined and mastered before proceeding to the next step.

3. Turning the switch on.

Do not begin this training step until your dog can be directed to place her front paws up on the wall within muzzle distance of the switch. Bear in mind throughout this training that a dog can tire easily in this position.

To turn the switch on, have your dog nose it up.

Keep the training short and positive. Make a little progress and then change to some other trick that you've been working on.

To teach your dog to push the switch on, first encourage her just to touch it. Rub a piece of meat on the switch itself and have some meat on hand as your encouraging treat. You must keep the switch dry throughout the training to avoid any possibility of electrical shock. Position yourself right next to the switch and say your dog's name followed by the command *"Nose it."* Initially encourage her to grab a small treat held close to the switch itself. Repeat this exercise until your dog's nose moves quickly to the switch to get the treat.

Now, duplicate everything again, but this time have your fingers positioned at the switch without a treat. When your dog tries to find the treat and makes nose contact, flip up the switch turning on the light in the room. Praise and reward her. As soon as your dog is proficient at this, remove your empty fingers from the switch and tap the switch with your fingernail to encourage your dog into touching it. Again, as your dog touches the switch, flip it and reward. Over several training sessions, teach her to expect a treat every time she touches the switch, and give her the visual feedback by immediately flipping it on as if she did it. If you have a regression in the training, back up and repeat the previous steps.

As you progress, be prepared to make a big fuss the first five times your dog turns the light on by herself. Praise her enthusiastically and go play with her favorite toy. If your dog is touching the switch, ever so gently, without it ever flipping on, you need to help her. Very gently move her muzzle to nudge it and, of course, give her a treat. The key from this point on is to reward her with a treat every time she moves the switch at all. Wait until she's nudging it consistently before you begin rewarding only the better accomplishments.

Once your dog is turning on the light on her own, move away from the wall a few steps and practice it. You and your dog should be standing and facing the wall with the light switch. Say her name followed by either *"Go, nose it"* or *"Go, paws up, and nose it"* as you swing out your arm toward the switch. If your dog is jumping up on a chair first before turning on the light, use the command *"Go up, paws up, and nose it."* Over several training sessions, increase the distance you're able to send her.

4. Turning the switch off.

The easiest way for your dog to turn the switch off is to *paw* the switch. There is a training advantage to this since it involves sending your dog to the same switch and requesting a different command. This avoids the confusion of having to command your dog to push the switch up and then push it down. This concept would be very hard for her to understand and difficult for her to learn. She'll easily understand that she always *noses* the light up and on, and always *paws* it down and off.

Before you have your dog place her front paws up on the wall, teach her the *paw* command. Grab some treats and get her in a *sit* position. Say the command *"Paw,"* and encourage her to hand you her right paw and give her a treat. The target of her paw should be your right hand, since most people shake with their right hands. If necessary, use your left hand to help out by nudging your dog's paw out and up until it lands in your hand. As with all the other training you've learned, nudge just enough for her to succeed and receive a treat but gradually reduce your help as she figures it out.

Once your dog is giving you her paw consistently for a treat, repeat everything but this time withdraw your right hand as the target at the last minute. Immediately reward her as she paws the air. With repetition, your dog should hear the command *"Paw"* and start pawing. Now you're ready for the switch.

To teach your dog to *paw* the switch off, direct your dog to place her front paws up on the wall and position yourself right next to her. Delicately adjust her, if necessary, so that her right paw is directly below the switch. Say her name followed by the command *"Paw it."* Gently help the paw up the wall and guide it into pull-ing the switch down, then reward. You'll find that your dog's nails act as a rake that almost can't miss. This move will take a little getting used to, however. Since part of her weight is on that right paw, she'll have to transfer the weight to the other paw.

Repeat this training several times and then momentarily pause before helping her lift the right paw. Praise and encourage your dog when she paws anything on the wall. Later you can reward her for better aim. Remember that a light should be turned off in this process. Your dog will receive beneficial feedback from it.

Once your dog is turning the light switch off on her own, move away from the wall a few steps and practice it, just as you practiced turning the switch on. This time, however, say her name followed by either *"Go, paw it"* or *"Go, paws up, and paw it"* as you swing out your arm toward the switch. If your dog is jumping up on a chair first before turning on the light, use the *go up, paws up, and paw it* command. Over several training sessions, increase the distance you're able to send her.

Final Thoughts

Once you've finished the training, it should be safe to remove the protection from the wall. Your dog should be able to complete the trick without causing major damage. At the very least, remove the cardboard before guests come and you demonstrate

To turn the switch off, have your dog paw it down.

the trick. When you perform the trick for an audience, the less you say the smarter your dog will look. Repeat a helpful command only if your dog stops her attempt. However, you must do it immediately or your support will come too late to matter. If she balks at all, it probably means she wasn't quite ready for an audience. A little more practice and you'll have the illuminating experience you hoped for.

To further develop this trick, try it on a variety of switches around the house and at locations other than your home. You might put the cardboard up initially on every unfamiliar switch until your dog gets used to it. Until she's hit ten or so switches, each will be an adjustment for her.

When you have taught this trick, you will have a head start in teaching the trick found in Chapter 1.

Twig C.D., a five-year old miniature pinscher, paws her nose.

Chapter 4

Nose Job

Pawing her itchy nose.

It's nice to have a few tricks in your dog's repertoire that can be performed in a stationary position without any props. This cute trick can be done without props and in very limited space. In this trick your dog will use her paw to scratch her muzzle. She will rub your audience the right way with this performance—not to mention her nose! During the process she will also learn how to shake hands. This will be a nice by-product of the training, since everyone demands that any self-respecting dog that does tricks shakes hands!

In this trick, you will teach your dog to use her right paw to perform. As with other tricks, having her use her right paw each time will save her confusion as to which paw to use for which trick. The right was chosen because that is the paw people expect to see when a dog shakes hands. Other tricks benefit from this as well.

There are three behavior components in this trick:

1. The *sit* position.
2. Shaking hands.
3. Pawing the nose.

You should teach your dog the components one at a time. Wait to proceed to the next step until the previous one is mastered.

1. The *sit* position.

Please refer to Chapter 6, pages 39–41, for the training for this behavior component.

2. Shaking hands.

To teach your dog to shake hands with someone, grab some tasty treats and head for a room that's free from distractions. You will be teaching her to react to two verbal commands (*paw* and *shake*), and a hand signal. Many other tricks will benefit from her knowing the *paw* command. The *shake* command is commonly used by most people when they want a dog to shake hands. By teaching it to your dog, you'll be giving her a better chance to pick up on other people's wishes and impress them. Throughout the training, alternate the use of the *paw* and the *shake* commands so that she learns them both. The accompanying hand signal for *shake* is done by merely presenting your right hand to her with your palm up.

To begin the training, have her *sit* while you position yourself on the floor in front of her with some treats. Using the verbal command and hand signal simultaneously, gently brush her right leg forward with your left hand. You want to keep this paw airborne until her paw lands in the palm of your right hand. Don't allow her to put her paw down! Help her, if necessary, by moving the position of your outstretched hand signal a bit to allow her to succeed. Once she has succeeded, praise and reward her with a treat, then repeat the procedure. This should be child's play for her—or, more accurately, pooch play!

Once your dog is shaking hands well without any prodding from your left hand, there are a few more things to practice. Get her to respond quickly to both verbal commands. She should also react to the hand signal alone. Presenting either the right or left hand should also get the command across to her. With this training she'll shake hands with anyone presenting a target for her paw. You don't want her to be thrown off by a person saying, "Put it there, gal!"

Practice presenting the hand signal at different heights. Now is also a good time to enlist a volunteer or several of your cohorts to practice shaking hands with her. Coach them into providing her with a treat and a good scratch immediately after receiving her paw.

Last, and most important for teaching her to *paw* her nose, practice giving the hand signal off toward her left side. The point is to try to get her paw to graze her muzzle as it heads toward your palm.

3. Pawing the nose.

With this behavior component, it is important for you to reward even the slightest progress or improvement. Expect this stage to take many training sessions. Be patient. You'll see progress.

To teach your dog to *paw* her nose, have her shake hands while you give the *shake* hand signal off toward her left side and say the verbal command *"Paw nose."* As with the previous training, get her paw to graze her muzzle as it heads toward your right palm. This time though, you will move your palm at the last second so that she doesn't receive a treat for hitting the target. If she's too quick for you, give her the treat that she deserves. Next time try to move your hand signal quickly off to the right to keep her from touching it.

You want to encourage your dog whenever her paw touches her muzzle. Watch closely and reward her immediately when she succeeds. To help her make the contact, use your left hand to control her muzzle. Hold it gently from below and aim it a little toward her right side and pointing down a bit. Control it in a way that doesn't block her vision or her ability

Have your dog in a sit position.

As you give the shake hand signal, gently control her muzzle from below.

As her paw makes contact with her muzzle, praise her and…

…reward her quickly.

to paw it. Now, use your right hand to give the hand signal off to her left side. Make sure the command is still in her field of vision. As her paw touches her nose each time, make a big deal out of it and instantly reward her. It is an advantage to keep a treat in the open right palm. The treat will keep her attention and, since your left hand will be busy with her muzzle, will allow you to get the reward to her quickly. If she regresses and won't lift her paw toward the hand signal, go back and review the earlier *shake* training.

Once your dog is successfully pawing her nose, you want to discontinue the use of the hand signal for *shake*. To do this, continue using the *paw nose* command, but make the *shake* hand signal less conspicuous each time. When the *shake* hand signal is no longer necessary, it is time to eliminate the use of your left hand in controlling the muzzle. This is easily accomplished by using your left hand to position her muzzle properly, then releasing it as you give the command. Reward her as she paws her muzzle, and repeat the training until you don't have to position her muzzle at all.

Now that your dog has the trick down, introduce the *paw nose* hand signal to the training. This hand signal is done using both the left and right hands. [Hold your right forearm vertically in front of you with your palm facing the left side. Allow your hand to flop to the left. If you are doing it correctly, your wrist should

The paw nose *hand signal.*
Left: The hand signal is made in a counter-clockwise circle.
Right: The left hand is stationary.

Left: Allow the back of your right hand to brush your left palm. Right: Continue the circular motion and repeat the hand signal.

now be bent with your palm facing the floor.] Keep the arm in this position as you brush the back of your right hand into the palm of your left. Try to brush it in a circular motion, rather than back and forth. This will cause momentary contact between your hands and provide a clearer signal to her.

To perfect the trick, practice it at a greater distance from your dog and slowly increase the number of times she paws her nose before you give her a treat.

Final Thoughts

Your own creativity can add a lot of fun to this trick. Instead of demonstrating that your dog knows how to paw her nose, get more mileage out of the trick by asking her a question. As your audience looks at her, give her the hand signal. You'll want to think of a question that will provoke laughter from your audience as your dog paws her nose. It will be funnier if they don't see the trick coming. For example, you can ask your dog what she thinks of lima beans. After she paws her nose, your response could be, "Yeah, I think they stink too!" Any subject can be used in place of lima beans, depending on the makeup of your audience (and I'm not referring to the eye shadow they might be sporting).

When you have taught this trick, you will have a head start in teaching the tricks found in Chapters 6, 15, 17, 19, and 21.

Chapter 5
Lip Service
The kiss.

This is an often-taught trick because any dog can learn it in just a few short training sessions. In this trick your dog will travel to a specific person and give that person a kiss or lick. It's most effective when it's not used as a formal trick, but when the situation requires a smooch or is improved by one. The success of this trick hinges on not only your ability to control when your dog kisses, but also on how well you judge a person's wish to be kissed!

People generally fall into three categories: those that request a kiss, those that treasure a kiss if it's sincerely given, and those that reach for a handkerchief at the mere thought of one! With a little practice, you'll find that it's pretty easy, as well as very interesting, to categorize people. You can learn a lot about people by observing their interaction with your dog.

The people who typically request a kiss from a dog are usually testing to see if the dog knows how. They seem to care more about his training than about receiving his affection. Since they ask for it, knowing when to have your dog supply a kiss is easy.

The second category of people are those that treasure your dog's kiss.

They are typically very affectionate people—blatant dog lovers who will hug your dog and talk to him. These people believe that all dogs love them and are flattered if a dog showers them with kisses. With this group, there is an advantage in using a hand signal rather than a vocal command. It will make the kiss seem more spontaneous and the recipient will enjoy the kiss all the more.

The final category contains those who don't like being kissed by a dog at all. Maybe it reminds them too much of how their Aunt Martha slobbered over them when they were children! They're an easy bunch to pick out since they're not very friendly to your dog. These people seem to fear that your dog may jump up on them, drool on their outfit, or deliberately shed loads of hair on them. Previous experience with an overenthusiastic pooch may have created their concern. Play it safe and avoid having your dog get his licks in on this type of recipient.

Although this trick is more like a repeated lick than a kiss, we will be using the command *kiss* because it sounds more appealing. While most people will enjoy an affectionate kiss, few will want to be licked by a dog.

Also, depending on where your dog licks, people may find it offensive. It's important and socially acceptable for him to lick *only* a person's cheek just in front of the ear. Be careful not to reward him for anything else.

There are two behavior components in this trick:

1. The kiss.
2. The *come.*

The first is the essence of the trick itself. The second is what I call a major directive. It will be useful whenever your dog wanders away from the person he needs to kiss. It will also give him an idea who that lucky recipient is in a crowd.

1. The kiss.

To teach your dog to *kiss,* have your dog *sit* facing you in the corner of a room that is free from distractions. During the training, you will be positioned on the floor directly in front of him. This way you'll have his full attention and he'll be a captive student. Have with you several food items that have a good scent and an appealing taste to your dog. In addition, bring some kernels of his food or other tidbits to reward him. Rub a food item on the back of your hand and, as you present it to him, say the command *"Kiss."* As he licks your hand, praise him verbally with *"Good"* so that he knows that you're pleased. Most dogs will find this great fun and very rewarding. If your dog is slightly hesitant, reward him for any lick—no matter how slight—by immediately giving him a treat. If you are having trouble getting him to lick your hand at all, experiment by rubbing different tempting food items on your hand until you find one that works. Continue the practice until he repeatedly licks the back of your hand.

The next step is to command your dog to *kiss* the same hand without rubbing the food item on it first. After he stops licking it, immediately reward him with a treat. Repeat this many times until he is proficient at it. He should lick your hand approximately four times before you reward him with a treat. Of course, you can build up to that gradually by rewarding him for the first lick, then two licks, etc. Introduce the hand signal for *kiss* during this training. It is done by wiggling your index finger on the hand that's not being licked. Make sure you do it close to the area you want licked and keep it wiggling until you want him to stop. As with most training, if you are having any trouble, back up and review the previous training.

Once your dog has mastered licking the back of your hand, transfer the training to your cheek, right in front of your ear. Do this by rubbing the food item on this area and repeat the previous training procedure until you no longer need to rub the food item on your cheek to be kissed sufficiently.

The next step in the training involves recruiting different volunteers for your dog to *kiss.* Again, start the training by rubbing the food item on the volunteer's cheek until it's no longer needed. Make sure you practice the *kiss* in different locations, such as other rooms in the house, the park, and when visiting other homes. Also, get your volunteers to turn the other cheek, since it is important that he will *kiss* either cheek. Treat your volunteers nicely. The job can get old quickly!

Practice the *kiss* enough so that your dog doesn't need to be rewarded with a treat every time he is requested to *kiss.* Substitute praise for the treat and only reward him with a treat occasionally.

2. The *come.*

For purposes of this trick, upon hearing the command *"Come, kiss"* your dog should immediately travel toward you and kiss the designated person. In this trick, the *come* com-

Put your dog on a stay. Attach a rope to the training collar.

Move about 10 feet away.

Call your dog and pull gently on the rope.

Guide your dog into a straight sit.

mand is used to guide him toward you so that he can find the right person to kiss. You'll find it handy in a crowd or whenever he has wandered away from the person desiring a kiss. Merely stand by the person in question and call your dog with *"Come, kiss."* As an alternative, you can call him with the *come* command and as he shows up, give him the hand signal for *kiss.* This works well since the person's attention will be on the dog and not on you.

To prepare training for the *come,* get a clothesline-sized rope approximately 25 feet in length and attach it to your dog's collar. Start the training by placing him in the *sit* position. If he moves, tell him *"No"* and put him back in the *sit* position. Go ten feet from him and stand facing him. Hold the rope in both hands and have it almost taut. Have a piece of food ready to reward him. Call him by saying his name followed by the command *"Come."* As he is coming toward you, pull up the slack in the rope so that you can control him. At the same time, back up in a straight line so that he wants to chase you. Be sure to praise him throughout this whole process. Try this several times and increase the distance of the *come.* When he has the command down pat, remove the rope and try it again. If he fails to come immediately when called, reattach the rope for a few more repetitions before trying it off-leash again.

Now that your dog has mastered the *come,* practice the *come, kiss* command. Use different volunteers and allow your dog to wander away from you before calling him. He'll pick it up quickly! Once the *come, kiss* command is learned, you can lengthen the command so that it sounds more conversational and normal by saying *"Come,* give 'em a *kiss."* When doing this, try to emphasize the two key words in the sentence.

Final Thoughts

The *kiss* hand signal is a wonderful tool to make a kiss appear sincere. It can be easily given to your dog without the person knowing. If you time it correctly, the person being kissed will feel special and honored. The signal can be your secret, since it's impossible for your dog to kiss and tell!

Chapter 6
No-How
The "no" headshake.

Upon hearing a question, your dog will respond by shaking her head "no." It will convey the message that she denies, refuses, or disagrees with your question. She wants to notify the know-it-all that she has nobility and that she is in no way a know-nothing nobody—just in case you had that notion! Your audience is sure to laugh if you use an appropriate question. All will be in awe that your dog has such human-like ability.

You'll need to think up some questions that will provoke a laugh after your dog shakes her head. It will be funnier if your audience doesn't see the trick coming. For example, tell everybody that when you got up this morning and opened the refrigerator, it almost looked like there were paw prints on the lower shelf. Then ask your dog, "Did you get up for a snack last night?" Your imagination will provide you with many good questions that she can respond to. Think along the lines of human-like behavior. Two examples might be whether she adds too much salt to her cooking, or if she has taken the trash out yet. Your own creativity can add a lot of fun to this trick.

The trick is an easy one to teach, since your dog shakes her head naturally in everyday life. She knows how to do it. You just need to train her to do it on command! You need to duplicate the things in nature that cause her to shake her head, then link them to the verbal command and hand signal.

There are two behavior components in this trick:

1. The *sit* position.
2. The headshake.

The *sit* is one of the major body positions a dog can assume. It is easiest for your dog to learn this trick from the sitting position. It is also the most attractive position from which to demonstrate the trick. After you've completed a short training lesson on sitting, you can teach the second component.

1. The *sit* position.

The *sit* is a position dogs use to enable themselves to rest their haunches while supporting themselves with their front legs. Once the

Left: Practicing the sit *command.*
Right: If your dog begins to break the stay...

Left: ...correct her by pushing her back toward the orginal spot.
Right: Help her into the sit position...

Left: ...by pushing down on her rear while pulling up on her training collar.
Right: Repeat the stay *command.*

sit command is given, your dog should remain in the *sit* position forever, theoretically, until released by you with the command *"Okay."* For this reason, when a longer *sit* is necessary, use her name followed by the command *"Sit! Stay!"* Using the *stay* command will reinforce the idea that she shouldn't budge. The *sit,* though a semiresting position, can be a very boring command if a dog is left in that position too long. A bored dog is tired, unhappy, and unacceptable! Keep yours excited about training by keeping the lessons short.

To train your dog for the *sit,* find an area for training that is free from distractions, and bring along some tasty treats for her. She already uses the position so all you have to do is teach her to assume the *sit* when you give the command. Start by using her name followed with the command *"Sit."* If she doesn't move immediately to a *sit* position, guide her gently but quickly into one. Then release her and reward her. A training collar and leash can be used to help guide her. If you do use one, merely pull up on the collar while pushing down on her rear. Initially, the *stay* command should be added to reinforce the fact that she should remain in that position. Continue this exercise for several days until she responds quickly to the command.

Once your dog has learned the *sit* command, increase your distance from her and practice. Find the greatest distance where you still have control, then slowly increase that dis-

The head *hand signal.*
Start off with your palms down.

Turn your palms up and push them out to the side...

...while shrugging your shoulders.

tance over many sessions. It is crucial that you correct her if she moves. Quickly guide her back into the same spot and give the command *"Stay!"* Remember, always allow your dog to succeed! She will progress much faster if you do.

2. The headshake.

To teach your dog the headshake, you will have to duplicate the things in nature that cause her to shake her head, such as a gentle breeze or a tickling near her ear. When you find something that works, you'll need to link it to the verbal command and hand signal. Expect to get only about five headshakes out of her in a session. This is a difficult reaction to stimulate. If you have found several methods that cause her to shake her head, by all means use them all to prolong the training! As soon as you notice that she is slow to react to any particular method, switch to another or stop. You want to keep her reacting to the method you've found, without making her immune to it and inadvertently training her not to react.

There are several things that you can try that will cause your dog to shake her head. A very effective method is to lightly blow in her ear from about a foot away. You can also try tickling the hairs of her ear with your finger or a feather. Another method is to loosely attach a large paper clip or similar device to one of her ears. Make sure the clip isn't pinching and causing pain. The clip should make her feel like a big bug just landed on her ear. If all else fails, use a squirt bottle to lightly mist an ear with water. It'll work, but it might not be her favorite! Remember a dog's ears are extremely sensitive. Be careful not to do anything that might cause pain.

Once you have found what causes your dog to shake her head, start linking the action to the commands. You will be using both the verbal command and the hand signal each time before you cause your dog to shake her head. It is very important to use every means you have to communicate your desire since you're dealing with an unknown number of times you can get her to repeat this action. For the verbal command, use her name first followed by the command *"Head."* The hand signal for *head* is done by having the palms of your hands turn up and push out to the side away from your body with a shrug of your shoulders. It's the typical gesture people use when they are unsure of an answer. Place your dog in a *sit*. Use both the verbal and hand signal commands simultaneously, cause her head to shake, and reward. The type of reward should be geared to the difficulty of getting her to shake her head. If it's no problem, use a treat and praise her. If you are having difficulty getting each headshake, make a bigger deal out of her success. Give her a treat, and then present her with her favorite toy and play with her for a minute. As with all your training, encourage, encourage! And, don't forget to encourage!

Through repetition she will learn the headshake quickly. To perfect the trick, make sure you practice both the verbal command and the hand signal separately, so that each form of the command will work for her. Also, practice with her in a standing and lying down position, and take her to different locations to practice so that she's ready for any situation.

Final Thoughts

For demonstration purposes, use only the hand signal as you ask your dog an appropriate question. You will find that after repeating the trick many times, you can actually make the hand signal less obvious. She can also be cued to shake her head by asking your question in a more theatrical way. Just overemphasize the question a bit. For a formal dinner, have her call your guests to the table by responding to the command while holding a bell. It's a terrific way to really put on the dog for your friends!

When you have taught this trick, you will have a head start in teaching the tricks found in Chapters 4, 15, 17, 19, and 21.

Chapter 7

Open and Shut Case

Retrieving an item from a drawer.

In this trick your dog will walk to a drawer, open the drawer, remove an item, deliver it to you, and return to push the drawer closed. The trick will be impressive. You will find it also practical and fun. It will allow your dog to help out around the house, whenever you need a helping paw.

There are four behavior components in this trick:

1. Pulling the drawer open.
2. Retrieving an item.
3. Delivering an item.
4. Pushing the drawer closed.

Each component should be taught independently. Once you've completed a short training lesson on one, you can start the training of another in the same session.

Choco C.D., C.R.T.I, a five-year-old Bouvier des Flandres, cleans up with this trick.

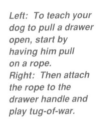

Left: To teach your dog to pull a drawer open, start by having him pull on a rope.
Right: Then attach the rope to the drawer handle and play tug-of-war.

Left: Next, have him pull the rope without your intervention.
Right: Slowly reduce the length of the rope by cutting it.

The end result.

1. Pulling the drawer open.

First, find the most suitable drawer in your home. You want to make it as easy as possible for your dog, so pick a drawer that slides easily and is at his mouth's height when he is in a standing position. The drawer needs to have a handle or knob on it. Damage may occur to the handle over time, but replacement handles are usually easy to find at your local building supply store. Usually the ideal drawer will be found in the kitchen and this area is perfect for future demonstrations since guests tend to gravitate toward it. For many reasons, it is best to empty the drawer during the initial training.

Start by teaching your dog to *pull.* Since the initial training does not require the use of a drawer, practice in a carpeted area so that your dog will have good footing. Grab an old sock and play with him. Once he's having a ball with his new toy, switch the game into a tug-of-war. Pull only as hard as he pulls, and repeat the command, *"Pull"* each time. Many dogs will growl, so don't be alarmed. It's usually a friendly growl they enjoy making while playing.

Once you've had a few great play sessions with the sock, try using a two-foot piece of soft rope. Tie several knots in the rope to help your dog grip it. Once you succeed in getting him to *pull* on it and to accept it as a toy, attach the rope to the drawer handle. Tell him to *"Pull it,"* and, if necessary, grab the portion of the rope near the handle. Play tug-of-war as if nothing had changed. Frequently use the release command *"Okay"* to get him to stop pulling and then reward your dog with a small treat. Work at getting him to grab and pull on the rope every time you command him to, and then immediately release and reward him.

Over several training sessions, slowly reduce the length of the rope by cutting it, until the rope no longer exists and your dog pulls on the handle itself. Also, strive toward having him pull the drawer out at least halfway before you reward him. Remember to work at his pace. Keep the training sessions short and very positive.

There are two reasons to avoid pulling with your dog. If he tends to be aggressive with people, pulling might cause the problem to become worse. It could encourage him to compete with you for the pack-leader job. It's important that you remain the undisputed alpha-leader of your small pack. Also, if your dog is still a puppy, put off training him to pull until he matures a bit. Puppies' teeth can be damaged by pulling too strenuously.

2. Retrieving an item.

The preliminary training for the retrieve is covered in Chapter 18, page 106. Once your dog is picking up his favorite toy regularly, open the empty drawer, toss it in, and repeat the command enthusiastically. If your dog is a little timid, coax him into grabbing his toy. If necessary, reach your hand into the drawer and elevate the toy so that your dog only needs to stick his muzzle in a bit. In all new training, try to take him one small step at a time.

Once the retrieve is mastered using your dog's toy, practice the retrieve with a variety of easily held items. To jazz up the trick, you'll want him to retrieve an item that your audience will appreciate. Consider using items such as a twenty dollar bill on the outside of a fake money roll, a rubber chicken, or maybe even a large dog cookie that you will allow him to eat at the end of the trick.

3. Delivering an item.

Please refer to Chapter 18, pages 108–110, for the training for this behavior component.

4. Pushing the drawer closed.

To teach your dog to push the drawer closed, first encourage him to touch the handle-end of the drawer. Rub his favorite odor on the drawer, just to the right of the handle. (My dogs like filet mignon, but I use a piece of hot dog or roast beef!) Position yourself right next to the drawer and say your dog's name followed by the command *"Come, nose it."* As he approaches, hold a little piece of the meat in the scented area and allow him to grab it off the face of the drawer. Repeat this exercise until your dog moves quickly over to the drawer to get the treat.

Now, duplicate everything again, but this time have your fingers positioned on the drawer front without the meat. When your dog comes up to grab it and makes nose contact with your fingers, praise and reward him with a treat using your other hand. As soon as your dog is consistent at this, remove your empty fingers from the front and, if necessary, tap the face of the drawer with your fingernail to encourage your dog to touch it. Over several training sessions, teach your dog to expect a treat every time he runs up and touches the drawer with his nose. If you have a regression in the training, back up and repeat the previous steps.

As you progress in training your dog to push the drawer, it becomes more important that he runs up perpendicular to the drawer's face. This can be accomplished by placing him in a *sit* before giving him the command *"Come, nose it."* As your dog runs toward the drawer to touch it, his momentum will nudge the drawer closed slightly. You want to encourage him verbally when he nudges the drawer. Make a big deal out of it and get him excited. You can also very gently help his muzzle to nudge it

Here the trick is wonderfully demonstrated using a drawer that's higher than recommended. This height requires the dog to place his paws up on the drawer or the counter top. It's easier if you choose a drawer that is at the height of your dog's mouth or a little lower.

and, of course, give him a treat. The key from this point on is to reward him with a treat every time he pushes the drawer in acceptably. Base this on the distance he's nudged it in previous attempts. Help your dog, if necessary, so that he succeeds each time and earns his reward.

Once he is pushing the drawer in on his own, move away from the drawer a few feet and practice it again. Have your dog next to you and facing the drawer. Issue the command *"Go nose it"* as you swing out your arm toward the drawer face. Over several training sessions increase the distance you send him.

Combining the Steps

As soon as your dog's training has progressed well with each of the components of the trick, combine the training as a unit. You'll find there is less chance of boredom setting in and your training sessions will be more productive than ever.

Get your dog to pull the drawer out using the shortened rope and give him a treat while praising. Then, tell him to *"Get it."* If necessary, gently direct him back toward the article and assist him if required. Once he has grabbed the article, give him the command *"Come, bring it."* Now reward him for the steps you've combined and tell him to *"Go, nose it."* Again, give him a treat when he has nosed it acceptably.

When your dog is fairly close to mastering all the different steps of this trick, require him to complete the entire combination of steps in order to get the food reward. Talk to him a lot through this stage. Tell him what to do and praise him as he completes the steps.

Final Thoughts

For performance purposes, the less you say the better. Talk him through a step of the trick only if he's having trouble. To advance the trick even more, try it on a variety of drawers and at different locations other than your home. Your audience will be in awe. For your dog, it will definitely be a moving experience!

When you have taught this trick, you will have a head start in teaching the tricks found in Chapters 1, 12, 14, 16, 18, and 22.

Chapter 8

Catchy

Catching water from a squirt gun.

U pon seeing a narrow stream of water being shot from your toy squirt gun, your dog will stick to his guns and aim to catch it! The audience will delight in his antics and share in his excitement. Your dog will

Tenzing, a four-year-old Lhasa Apso, catches water from a squirt gun.

need to catch that squirt or get wet. He'll either be a hit or get hit!

This trick has lots of advantages. Chances are you already own a squirt gun. If you don't, you can purchase one at a low cost. The squirt gun, being small and easy to carry, is an ideal prop compared to many others. It is also easy to perform this trick in a very limited space. If that's not enough, your dog will consider the training for this trick more like a game and thoroughly enjoy every session. Best of all, he'll be quick to "catch" on!

Your dog is bound to make a splash with this trick! I mean this literally, so you need to initially pick an area that won't be harmed by the water. Remember, it's not just the water from one session but the water from the many sessions required in the training of this trick that can do some harm. Once the trick is learned, possible water damage still should be a consideration, but to a lesser extent. During a performance, ten squirts of your gun and ten fabulous catches by your dog should limit your water problems.

There are two behavior components in this trick:

1. Catching kernels of dog food.
2. Catching water shot from a squirt gun.

The first is a very practical one for your dog to know. It can be utilized in all the dog training you do in the future. It gets the reward to him quickly, when it is most effective. It should be taught first before you teach the second behavior component.

1. Catching kernels of dog food.

The word *catch* will tell your dog that you are going to throw something to him and that you want him to catch it. It does carry with it a certain trust that must never be broken. Ask him to catch only those items that are completely safe for him to catch. His eyesight limits his ability to discern whether you are tossing a rock or a piece of food. Build his trust in you by being as faithful to him as he is to you.

Dogs vary greatly in their natural ability to catch things, but all dogs can be trained to do better than they would without training. Training involves throwing small kernels of dog food to your dog. Get him to lie down about five feet away from you, and toss him a piece of food. Keep your tosses gentle, and initially aim at his mouth. When he succeeds in catching the food almost every time, angle your throws slightly to the side. Increase the challenge as he improves.

Gently toss a kernel of dog food.

Initially aim at his mouth.

Increase the challenge as he improves.

Build his catching ability slowly, always allowing him to catch more than he misses by adjusting the difficulty of your throws. Say the command *"Catch!"* and make the toss. He will learn the word *catch* quickly because he will know that something enjoyable is coming his way—by air mail no less! If his attention is not on you when you want him to catch something, say his name first, followed by *"Catch."*

A game of catch will improve your dog's "eye-mouth" coordination. This game will also help cure the dog that allows the kernel to drop to the floor before eating it. To play the game, have your dog lie down and position yourself on the floor in front of him. As before, use the *catch* command and make the toss. This time if he drops the food, quickly grab it and repeat the process. He'll quickly learn that he needs to catch that treat or miss the opportunity to eat it!

Once your dog has the *catch* mastered while lying down, practice it when he is sitting and standing. Also, work on increasing the distance you toss the kernel. Practice the *catch* in different locations and with different distractions will perfect his skills.

2. Catching water shot from a squirt gun.

To teach your dog to catch water shot from a squirt gun, use the same training techniques you used to teach him to catch kernels of dog food. Get him to lie down about five feet away from you on "waterproof" flooring, and warm him up by tossing a few kernels. Then, say the command *"Catch!"* and fire a single shot from the squirt gun. Try to aim at his mouth and avoid his eyes, if possible. He'll be gun-shy at first and unsure of what you are doing. You need to ease the shock of that squirt coming, so that he doesn't find it offensive. To do this, follow each squirt of the gun instantly with the feedback command *"Good!"* and hand him a few kernels. Return to tossing the kernels several times, and then try the squirt gun again. Repeat this process until he opens his mouth for the first time to catch the water spray. It doesn't matter if he catches it or not, the attempt is what's important! As soon as he makes this first attempt, make a big deal out of it. Lavish praise and some kernels of dog food on him. Stop your training session and go do something that he considers a big reward, like playing ball.

As you pick up the training in your next session, repeat the process of throwing kernels to your dog and periodically shooting your squirt gun at him for him to catch the water. Remember to praise each of his attempts at catching the water, and instantly reward him by handing him some kernels. Once he attempts to catch every squirt from the gun, you can slowly phase out the food tossed in between squirts. This procedure acts as conditioning that allows him to transfer his knowledge of catching the kernels of dog food to catching the stream of water from the gun.

Make sure you don't jump the gun! Wait until your dog is attempting to catch every squirt of the gun for a treat before you eliminate the food toss. Then reward him only for successful catches and not just the attempts. This will heighten his skills in catching the squirt. At this point, you can also start to toss him the reward he gets for catching the squirt, instead of having to hand it to him each time. You can now begin to slightly angle your squirts above, below, and to each side. Increase the challenge as he improves. As with the kernel catching, build his catching ability slowly, always allowing him to catch more than he misses by adjusting your shots.

You are now ready to shape this behavior into the trick. To do this, you will slowly increase the number of squirts your dog catches before being rewarded. Start by having him *catch* two squirts before rewarding him. After some practice, work on three squirts, four squirts, etc. Also practice having him in the standing, sitting, and lying down positions. One of them will best complement the trick

for a demonstration. Most dogs will look best in the standing position.

Final Thoughts

Experimentation and your good judgment will be the key. You'll have to decide how many times to shoot your dog with the squirt gun when demonstrating this trick. Each dog will do it differently. Some dogs will lose their enthusiasm after several squirts, whereas others are having such a good time growling and jumping around that ten squirts might not be enough. Be careful not to bore your audience with the same thing for too long. Also, unless your dog looks like he is having fun, a portion of your audience might think that you're being mean if you overdo it. I keep the trick to about seven rapid-fire squirts. I'm left with a dry, attractive dog and an audience that wants a little bit more. Trust me, there's no catch. Your dog will enjoy the trick because he'll come across looking more like a big gun than a little squirt!

When you have taught this trick, you will have a head start in teaching the trick found in Chapter 21.

Tillie, an eight-year-old wirehaired fox terrier/airedale, crawls along the ground.

The down command. Left: Give your dog the down command. Right: Guide the dog…

Left: …into the down position. Right: Give the stay command.

Chapter 9
Getting the Low Down
Crawling along the ground.

This is one of the traditional tricks covered in this book. It's a popular trick because any dog can learn it in just a few short training sessions. What people don't realize is that the basic trick can be advanced to a higher level (or should I say a lower level!) with just a little extra work.

The crawl is a movement your dog will make by creeping along the ground with her chest remaining in contact with it. Dogs will crawl naturally when they want to reach a close item. This natural ability accounts for the ease of the training. Increasing the distance of the crawl makes the trick more exciting to an audience.

There are three behavior components in this trick:

1. The *down* position.
2. Food leading.
3. The crawl.

The *down* is one of the major body positions a dog can assume. Your dog will need to start out, and remain, lying down throughout the training for the crawl. After you've completed a short training lesson on it, you can proceed to teach the other components.

In teaching the crawl…

…tempt your dog to stretch for the food.

Use your other hand to keep her in the down position. Eventually, allow her to reach the tidbit.

55

1. The *down* position.

The *down* is a position in which your dog is on the floor with her hind legs under her and her front legs extended. Your dog already lies down naturally. All you have to do is teach her to assume the position when you give her the command.

To teach her the *down* command, get your dog into a *sit* position. Give the command *"Down,"* then guide her into lying down by grabbing her front paws and gently sliding them out in front of her. You might have to use your other hand to keep her rear from trying to rise up. Be sure to reward and praise her. Once the *down* command is given, she should remain in the *down* position forever, theoretically, until released by you with *"Okay."* Repeat this several times but pause slightly after giving the *down* command to give her a chance to comply without your help. In just a few short training lessons, she should have the command down pat. Go slowly and keep it very positive. Make a big fuss over her the first time that she assumes a *down* position on command without your help. Your excitement means everything!

Throughout the training of this trick, whenever your dog breaks out of the *down* position, immediately correct her. Give her the command to *down,* help her back into the position if necessary, and praise her before returning to the lesson.

2. Food leading.

Please refer to Chapter 13, pages 74–75, for the training for this behavior component.

3. The crawl.

A crawl is easily achieved by first giving your dog the command *"Down."* Position yourself on the floor next to and slightly ahead of her. Use her name followed by the command *"Come, crawl."* The *come* command will help communicate to her that she should move toward you. Hold a piece of food in your hand and tempt her into stretching forward for it. Use your other hand to gently keep her in the *down* position if she attempts to get up. Allow her to succeed in reaching the food, but require her to reach a little farther each time. In the *crawl,* she needs to shift her front paws to move forward and scoot her hindquarters along. If necessary, you can help her by moving one paw at a time so that she gets the idea and also the food reward! She should be crawling on her first lesson.

Tapping the floor with the food works well as a hand signal. It directs your dog's eyes to the lowest point and encourages her to stay down. This hand signal is also an advantage for future demonstrations of the trick. It will look more professional if you use only the verbal command *"Crawl"* once and do not have to repeat it over and over.

To advance the *crawl,* you need to position yourself a short distance out in front of your dog and give her the command. Increase your distance slightly after she succeeds with the previous distance. It is important to go slowly. If you increase this distance too fast, you'll encourage her to fail. As you get farther away from her, it will be harder to make a correction. She'll be up and moving before you have a chance to get to her. She will test you! Being prepared to act in the proper way will benefit you in minimizing future corrections. At the very moment she begins to leave the *down* position, yell *"No"* to stop her in her tracks. Follow this quickly with the *down* command and praise her verbally for listening to you. Then, return to the hand signal directing her to *crawl.*

The longer the crawl, the more impressive it will be. If you are having trouble with the longer distances, you may have proceeded too fast with the training. Go back to the beginning and review it. If this fails, try having an assistant tailgate your dog to help keep her end down. If an assistant is not an option, you can try some boards raised across her path. Use some boxes to support them so that she'll have to remain in the *down* to go underneath them.

Final Thoughts

To advance this trick even further, use the previously described techniques to teach your dog to crawl up and down steps. After she has mastered this and you get her to perform it for an audience, she'll have something over you—she'll have proven she can maintain a low profile!

When you have taught this trick, you will have a head start in teaching the tricks found in Chapters 11, 13, 15, 23, and 25.

Chapter 10
Well-Balanced
Walking with a book balanced on her head.

In years gone by, all proper little girls practiced walking while balancing a book on their heads. They wanted to learn to walk with poise and grace. In this trick your dog will show that she has her head on straight! You will balance a book on your dog's head and back up ten feet or so. On your signal, she will walk slowly to you while keeping the book balanced. Most of your audience will have unsuccessfully tried this balancing act themselves and will appreciate the difficulty involved in perfecting this trick!

This trick looks a lot harder than it is. The top of most dogs' heads provides a small, flat surface on which a book can be easily balanced. The trick is accomplished by controlling the position of your dog's head so that she can *keep* the book balanced.

Tundra U.D., the author's Samoyed, balances a book on her head. Perform the trick so that it can be viewed from the dog's side. This will make the most of each slow step.

People will be impressed with you for raising such a level-headed dog!

Just about any book will work for the trick, but you should avoid those with glossy covers. A hardback book works well if you remove its jacket. Keep in mind, too, that a Dachshund might have a hard time handling a copy of Shakespeare's complete works! Experiment to find the right book. You want one that is easy for your dog to balance, yet gives the impression of genuine difficulty.

The color of the book should contrast with your dog's coat so that it is seen easily by your audience. Occasionally someone will be curious as to your dog's reading selection. Try to pick a title that encourages their laughter. Of the dog books in print, *From Riches to Bitches* or *Astrology for Dogs* would do nicely. My favorite is *The Intelligent Dog's Guide to People-Owning,* unfortunately now out of print. Many funny titles can be found by searching a used bookstore.

There are four behavior components in this trick:

1. The *stand* position.
2. Walking slowly.
3. Balancing a book while standing.
4. Balancing a book while walking.

The first three components should be taught independently. Once you've completed a short training lesson on one, you can begin training the others in the same session. Wait until these three are learned before proceeding to the fourth component.

1. The *stand* position.

Please refer to Chapter 22, pages 124–125, for the training for this behavior component.

2. Walking slowly.

To teach your dog to walk slowly you will need some tasty treats, a long leash, and an assistant's help. Begin by placing your dog in a *stand*. Issue the command "*Stay*" while giving her the *stay* hand signal. This hand signal is performed with the hand open, palm facing the dog. Your fingers can be pointing to the side, down, or up. Whenever you give her the *stay* command, it is important that you correct her if she moves. Immediately put her back into the original position and repeat the command. The *slow* hand signal is a variation of the *stay* hand signal. It consists of starting with the *stay* hand signal, holding it momentarily, then closing your fingers into a fist momentarily, and then repeating this sequence over and over.

To begin teaching your dog to walk slowly, attach the leash to her collar and have your assistant stand behind her, holding the leash. Position yourself on the floor in front of her, and display the *stay* hand signal. Give her the command "*Slow*" as you close up the hand signal into a fist. It may be necessary to use the command "*Come, slow*" at first, tempting her into moving until she gets the idea. As she moves forward, instantly spread out your fingers again into the *stay* hand signal while your assistant gives a gentle tug on the leash to stop the dog's forward movement. Reward your dog with a treat and repeat the training, moving across the room one step at a time. Your assistant's job is to control your dog's forward movement by gently tugging the leash every time the assistant sees you put up the *stay* hand signal. Your assistant is your watchdog. Your dog should take one step and freeze, awaiting a treat and further orders from you. It is important to release your dog when you reach the other side of the room or finish the practice. Do this by using the *okay* command and praising her.

Once your dog is good at taking one step at a time, allow her to decide when to pause without receiving a warning tug. Your assistant should still be on duty in case your dog needs a correction for not complying with your orders. When this occurs have your assistant say *"No!"* and give a gentle tug on the leash at the same time. Practice until your dog is good at taking one step at a time, and your assistant is no longer needed. The next stage requires that your dog take a step and stop, and another step and stop before getting her treat. Extend this until she can step and then stop two times before you reward her. Increase to three times and then four times before you reward her. Practice until you can control her

slow walk for approximately ten feet. (See photos on page 132.)

(See photos on page 132.)

3. Balancing a book while standing.

It is an easy process to teach your dog to balance a book on her head while standing still. Have her *stand* while you place the book on her head. Control her muzzle as you do this. Quickly remove the book and reward her with a treat. As she gets used to the book, lengthen the time you require her to have it on her head. Through this stage, continue to control her muzzle, thereby making it impossible for her to lose balance of the book. Now, repeat the exercise, but this time give the *stay* hand signal you learned when teaching her to walk slowly and release your hold on her muzzle momentarily. Your dog should stare at your *stay* hand signal until you remove the book with your other hand. Very gradually build up the time your dog will balance the book, and reward her with a treat each time for her success. You'll find that her nose will tend to drift either up or down. Encourage her to look at your open hand by tapping it with the fingers from your other hand. If her nose is drifting up, you can effectively compensate by lowering your hand signal. Likewise, if her nose is drifting down, move your hand signal higher. Throughout your practice, if the book slides off her head, tell her *"No!"* and begin again. If this is happening of-

Gently control your dog's muzzle while you give her the stay hand signal.

ten, it probably indicates that you are proceeding too quickly with the training. Go slowly and allow her to succeed, thus building confidence. In the long run you will find that it is always best to proceed at the pace your dog can handle.

4. Balancing a book while walking.

Wait to teach this behavior component until the others have been mastered. This component combines those separate behaviors and utilizes the same training techniques. If you are having any trouble with the training here, back up and review the preceding behavior components.

To begin training your dog to balance the book while walking, have her *stand,* balance the book on her head, and give her the *slow* hand signal. Utilize the same techniques you learned earlier to advance her one step. As soon as she takes one step, grab the book off her head, and reward her with a treat. Try to keep her head level by holding your hand signal at the right height. Be constantly aware whether the book is balanced

Release your hold on her muzzle. Gradually increase the time she balances the book.

or not and of any adjustments you need to make in your hand signal. Practice, over and over, until it is easy for her to take one step while keeping the book balanced. Once she has mastered this, work on having her take two steps, and then three, etc., until she can balance the book step after step for at least ten feet.

Final Thoughts

Once your dog is taking four or five steps toward you while balancing the book, you're ready for a performance. You'll find that the trick looks its best when viewed from the dog's side. This way your audience can watch her take each slow step and appreciate the difficulty involved. Even though your dog is balancing the books with ease, I'd refrain from firing your accountant. The IRS looks unfavorably on paw prints!

When you have taught this trick, you will have a head start in teaching the tricks found in Chapters 2, 13, 17, 20, 22, 24, and 25.

Chapter 11

On a Roll
Rolling over and back.

This trick proves, without a doubt, that your dog is the perfect roll model! In this traditional trick your dog will lie down and roll completely over. He will then quickly roll back in the other direction to his original position. Having him roll one way and back the other will make this old trick a fresh one for your audience. It will also show your dog's versatility. It's a perfect trick since no props are needed and it can be performed in a limited space. Best of all, your dog can learn it in a few short training sessions.

There are five behavior components in this trick:

1. The *down* position.
2. Food leading.
3. Lying on his side.
4. Rolling over.
5. Rolling back in the other direction.

Initially, each component should be taught independently. Once you've completed a short training lesson on one, you can start the training of another in the same session. However, your dog should master the fourth behavior component before you begin teaching him the fifth.

1. The *down* position.

Please refer to Chapter 9, page 56, for the training for this behavior component.

2. Food leading.

Please refer to Chapter 13, pages 74–75, for the training for this behavior component.

3. Lying on his side.

To teach your dog to lie on his side, grab some treats and position yourself on the ground facing him. Have him lie down on his stomach, helping him into position if necessary, and begin the training. You want to give the verbal command *"Side"* as you give the accompanying hand signal. The *side* hand signal is done using an open hand with the palm in front of and facing your body. The hand is then moved horizontally away from your body while flipping the palm up. The hand signal will communicate which side you want him to be lying

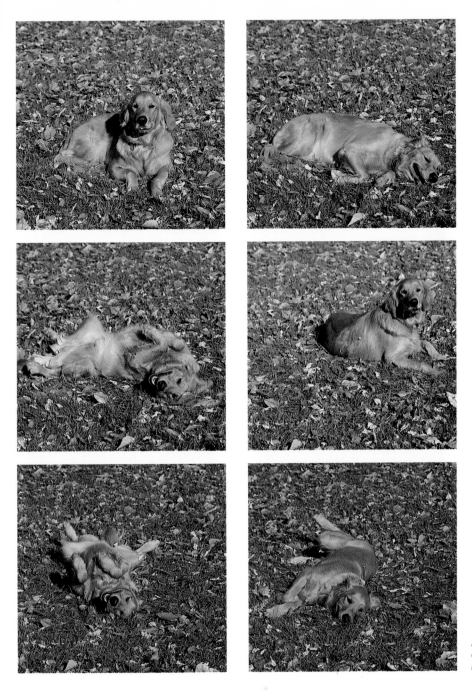

Andy, a nine-month-old golden retriever, rolls over and back.

on. Use your right hand when you want him on his left side and use your left hand when you want him on his right side. You are merely giving the hand signal in the direction that you want him to go.

To begin the training give your dog the verbal command and the hand signal simultaneously. Gently help him onto his side, and reward him with a treat. You'll find that if you use one hand to control his front legs and place the other on the side of his upper neck, you'll have perfect control in assisting him to his side. Repeat this process many times, pausing slightly after giving the commands to give him a chance to do it successfully on his own. Once he is doing it on his own, it's important that he remain on his side until you release him with the *okay* command. If necessary, use your hand to keep him from popping up. This will properly condition him for the future task of rolling over.

As soon as your dog is moving unassisted to both sides, it is time for you to practice the same exercise while you are standing. After your dog responds well close up, begin gradually increasing your distance from him. Over several sessions, he should be able to lie on either side from a minimum of ten feet away.

4. Rolling over.

To teach your dog to roll over, grab a supply of treats and position yourself on the ground facing him. Have him lie on his side, helping him into position if necessary, and begin the training. You want to give the verbal command *"Roll"* as you give the accompanying hand signal. The *roll* hand signal is done by making a one-foot diameter circle with your hand. Make the hand signal clockwise with your right hand if you want him to roll to your right. Go counterclockwise with your left hand to have him roll to your left. Initially, practice the *roll* to only one side to avoid confusing your dog. This will help the final product look sharp. When you practice the next behavior component he'll get practice rolling in the other direction. For purposes of explanation only, I will be instructing you on having your dog start out on his left side. Feel free to start him on his right side if you like.

To begin the training have your dog lie on his left side and give him both the verbal command and the hand signal. Immediately use your left hand to grab his front left leg (the leg nearest the ground). Grasp the upper portion, close to the shoulder. By controlling this leg you not only keep him from assuming the *down* position but you can also gently assist him in rolling over. Now is the time to utilize the food-leading techniques you've been practicing in another behavior component of this trick. Holding a treat in your right hand, encourage him to turn his head so that he is looking skyward. As you do this, gently help him roll over and reward him with the treat. You'll notice that this food-leading motion is very similar to the *roll* hand signal. As you practice more, require him to roll completely over and finish in the *down* position before rewarding him with a treat. As he becomes more accomplished, gradually eliminate the food leading and any help you give him. To phase out the food leading, do your tempting just a little farther away from his nose each time, eventually turning it into the *roll* hand signal.

Once your dog is rolling unassisted, it is time for you to perfect this skill. Practice using the vocal command and the hand signal separately. This will ensure that both the vocal command and the hand signal are mastered. Also, review all your training while you are in a standing position. When his response is sharp up close, gradually increase the distance. Over several sessions, you should be able to get your dog to roll when you are ten or more feet in front of him.

5. Rolling back in the other direction.

Your dog must know how to *roll* in one direction before you attempt to teach him to *roll* back in the other direction. If he doesn't have that mastered yet, wait to proceed with the training outlined here.

To teach your dog to roll in the other direction, follow the same techniques you used in teaching him to *roll* over. Instead of starting your dog on his left side, start him on his right. You will use your left hand to give a counterclockwise hand signal while your right hand is prepared to grab his right leg and assist him. It is not essential for him to master this now. Once he is doing it fairly well, you can work on the entire trick at the same time.

Combining the Steps

When your dog is performing each of the components of the trick well, combine the training as a unit. Start up close and sit on the ground in front of him. Say the command *"Down,"* then follow this with the *side* command and the hand signal. As soon as he makes the first move toward his side, throw in the *roll* command and hand signal. This will maintain his momentum and help him roll. You'll notice that you are using the same hand to do both the hand signals required. Allow them to flow together as one. The "job description" for the other hand is the same for both the *side* and *roll* commands—to keep the dog from making a mistake and to be there in case he needs a little help. As he rolls over into the lying-down position, hand him a treat and command him to lie on his other side. Again, as he initially moves toward his side, throw in the *roll* command and hand signal. Reward him

Teaching your dog to lie on his side.
Left: Give the verbal command and start the hand signal.
Right: Move your hand horizontally away from your body…

Left: …while flipping the palm up.
Right: Gently help him…

Left: …onto his side.
Right: Reward him with a treat.

with a treat as he returns to the position from which he began.

Once your dog is proficient at this, phase out the treat given on the first roll. Wait until he has rolled over and back before rewarding him. Again, as with the other training you've done, practice until he can do the trick when you command him from farther and farther away.

Final Thoughts

It is important that you use the *roll* command at the start of this trick to alert your audience to what your dog is supposed to do. Other than that one verbal command, try to stick to hand signals unless he stumbles and needs your help. Your audience is familiar with this trick and would judge any extra coaching as unnecessary. The trick is a winner because your dog rolls back the other way. Use the hand signal for the reverse roll. This gives you the opportunity to say anything you like. You can make him look smart by using a sentence like, "Head back from whence you came." You can try for a laugh by waiting until he has rolled back and suggest to your audience that his last move was a case of roll reversal!

When you have taught this trick, you will have a head start in teaching the tricks found in Chapters 9, 13, 15, 23, and 25.

Teaching the roll. Have your dog begin on his side.

Grab the leg nearest the ground.

Use a treat to encourage him to turn his head skyward. Gently help him roll over and...

...reward him with the treat.

Chapter 12

Drop in Often!
Dropping tennis balls into their can.

In this marvelous trick your dog retrieves several tennis balls, one at a time, and drops them into a tennis ball can. Other than the dogs I have personally worked with, I have seen only a pawful of dogs that were trained to make such a precise drop. This trick will show off the advanced training you and your dog have completed and will demonstrate just how smart your dog is. Your audience is guaranteed to find it unparalleled. You'll be proud and impressed, too!

The training is an easy progression of teaching your dog to drop the tennis balls into smaller and smaller boxes until she is accurate enough to hit the tennis ball can. If she is retrieving well already, you'll see daily progress as she gets more precise in dropping the balls in the can. The difficulty she has is that her muzzle greatly obstructs her view of the can below it. In lieu of cosmetic surgery, a little practice is all she needs!

You will need to prepare the tennis ball can before each training session and demonstration. Tape the can down so that it won't tip over when your dog drops the tennis balls in. Use small loops of masking tape (sticky side out) and place them on the bottom of the can. Be forewarned that masking tape can damage certain items. In most cases it won't, however, unless you leave it on for a long time. Plastic tennis ball cans have a cavity in the bottom that must be filled with additional tape. This will give the can a flatter bottom and more area to stick to the floor. Since the bottom of the plastic can is transparent, the masking tape will show. If this is objectionable to you, use transparent tape or paint the lower inch and bottom of the can. The old metal tennis ball cans were better because of their additional weight, flat bottoms, and ability to hide the tape. The clear plastic cans have one wonderful advantage, however. They let your audience know instantly whether or not your dog hits her target.

If you are practicing or performing outside on the lawn, masking tape won't work. You will need to drill a hole in the center of the can's bottom and insert a long nail through the hole to hold it steady. A pair of pliers will make it easy to slide the nail through the hole from the inside, then use a stick to push the nail into the ground. Another solution is to place a weight in the bottom of the can to steady it. Try sand, dirt, pennies, etc.

There are two behavior components in this trick:

1. Retrieving a tennis ball.
2. Dropping a tennis ball into a can.

Initially, each component should be taught independently. Once you've completed a short training lesson on one, you can start the training of another in the same session. Combine the training as soon as your dog is doing well on the retrieve.

1. Retrieving a tennis ball.

The preliminary training for the retrieve is covered in Chapter 18, page 106. Once the retrieve is mastered when using your dog's favorite toy, practice the retrieve with a tennis ball. She'll love it as a toy. The tennis ball is generally large enough so that she can't accidentally swallow or choke on it. Veterinarians are kept busy with the problems smaller balls often cause. There has been some recent health concern about the dye in tennis balls. Although you won't notice any of the dye bleeding off, a dog that chews on tennis balls supposedly is ingesting a minute amount. If you want to be safe, put the balls through your washer and dryer. If your dog chews on the balls or tears them up, they're probably not the best toy for her. If this is the case,

bring the tennis balls out only occasionally for play or when teaching this trick.

2. Dropping a tennis ball into a can.

To teach your dog to drop an item into a container, it is first necessary that you train your dog to hold an item. If she is already holding her favorite toy whenever you hand it to her, you'll only need to teach her the command *drop* and some movement. If your dog hasn't learned to hold an item, delay this training slightly until you've taught your dog the *get* command.

To teach your dog the command *drop,* find an article that would be uncomfortable for her to hold. The idea is to make her want to drop it badly enough so that dropping it will actually be a reward for her. Pick an object that she has a hard time holding. Since she will be dropping it, make sure your selection can't be damaged or won't damage the floor when dropped. You might try an egg whisk, a set of metal measuring spoons, or a cardboard box that is uncomfortable for her to hold.

With the proper article and some treats in hand, put your dog in a *sit* and have her *hold* the article. In an excited tone use your dog's name followed by the command *"Drop it!"* At the same time, offer her a treat and gently knock the article out of her mouth, praising her as you do so.

Fiona C.D. S.H., a seven-year-old Irish setter, drops a tennis ball into its can.

Repeat this exercise until she starts dropping the article on her own in order to eat the food you are offering. If you still have trouble, try waiting a longer period after giving the *drop* command, use an article less pleasing to hold, or offer her a treat so desirable that she can't help but drop the article to exchange it for the treat. She should catch on quickly.

When using the *drop* command, it is unwise to catch the article as your dog drops it. If you reach out to catch it, she will soon begin to hold it only until you reach out for it. Your reaching out will become a hand signal for her to drop the article. This will be undesirable when you want her to drop something far away from you with a verbal command only. You won't be there to give her a hand signal. In addition, if you send her to deliver an article to someone, you'll want her to hold it until the article is taken from her mouth.

Once your dog has caught on to the *drop* command, it is time to teach her the *go, drop it* command. Ideally, it is best to practice in a large, empty room that is free from all distractions.

Choose a large receptacle to catch the article to be dropped. If possible, place a sturdy, empty box in an unobstructed corner. The corner will direct your dog's attention to the box and also control her path of travel between you and the corner. To make the *drop* easy for your dog, the box needs to be about four inches lower than your dog's mouth when she is standing. If necessary, cut off the top few inches of the box.

Have your dog *sit* about one foot in front of the box and *hold* the article. Say your dog's name to get her attention and follow this with the command *"Go, drop it."* The command *go* helps her understand that you want her to move away from you. If she doesn't move, ease her into a *stand* while you support her jaw, with the article in it, from below. Allow the article to drop when her mouth is over the box. Reward your dog with a treat and a lot of praise.

Over several training sessions, practice with the box until she is proficient with increased distances and in different locations. You will also want her to start dropping a tennis ball, instead of the uncomfortable item, for all remaining training.

Once your dog has learned the *go, drop it* command, it is time to teach her to use smaller and smaller drop zones. Do this by using a slightly smaller box or container every training session. You will find that pots and pitchers will work well later in the training. Progress at her speed and reward her with a treat after each successful attempt. If she is having trouble with a particular size box, either back up in the training to the previous (larger) box, or remain at that box for several sessions until she has mastered it. The key is to go slowly and build her confidence by allowing her to succeed. When she misses, be prepared to command her to *"Get it"* and *"Go, drop it."* As the drop zone gets smaller, she is more likely to miss. She should hit her target on her first attempt 75 percent of the time. When she misses, she should be able to recover the tennis ball quickly and drop it in successfully. You'll be practicing with the tennis ball can before you know it!

Have your dog sit and hold *the article.*

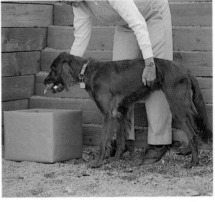

Ease her into a stand while you support her jaw. Allow the article to drop when her mouth is over the box.

Final Thoughts

Once your dog is able to drop the tennis ball in the can with ease, get her used to dropping two tennis balls before receiving a treat. This will make your performance a little longer and squelch any thought that she was just plain lucky on her first ball. Start by throwing out one tennis ball, wait for her to drop it successfully into the can, and then throw the second ball out. When you perform this trick for an audience, the less you say the smarter your dog will look. Repeat a helpful command only if your dog stops her attempts. Your dog's smashing success will definitely give her "the drop" on your audience!

When you have taught this trick, you will have a head start in teaching the tricks found in Chapters 1, 7, 16, and 18.

Chapter 13

Trying to Make Ends Meet

Chasing her tail.

This is another of the more popular tricks you may have seen demonstrated. It is a favorite of trainers because it is simple to teach. In this trick you will teach your dog to do what we've, unfortunately, all done on occasion—run around in circles! To add some pizazz to the trick, you'll have her reverse direction. This trick is guaranteed to make your audience giggle, especially if you preface it by saying, "This is her impersonation of a dog catcher!"

There are four behavior components in this trick:

1. The *stand* position.
2. Food leading.
3. Chasing the tail.
4. Reversing direction.

The *stand* is one of the major body positions a dog can assume. It will make it easier for your dog to learn the trick if she remains in this position. After you've completed a short training lesson on it, you can proceed in teaching the other components as long as you are aware that she needs to remain in the *stand*.

1. The *stand* position.

Please refer to Chapter 22, pages 124–125, for the training for this behavior component.

2. Food leading.

Many of the simplest tricks you can teach your dog require the use of a technique I call food leading. Food leading is a method of controlling your dog's movement by teaching her to follow a piece of food.

To teach food leading, grab a kernel of her food or another tidbit with all the fingertips of your hand. The food should be shielded from your dog so that she can't grab it. She might think you are handing her a piece of food, so you need to be cautious during the initial training to avoid being nipped accidentally due to her overenthusiasm. Proceed slowly and be prepared to correct any assault she makes. Yell *"No!"* and lightly shake her neck as a correction if she's being too aggressive. She shouldn't even be allowed to nudge your fingertips. Let her see the food, but you must be the one who decides when to give it to her. When you do decide, open your hand and allow her to eat the food from your palm. Once your dog understands that *you* control when the food is released, you can start leading her around by smoothly moving the hand that's holding the treat. Entice her into following it, then give her the treat. Gradually increase the distance you lead her. Her muzzle should follow about six inches behind your hand. You'll find that this is a convenient hand signal and that you'll use it whenever you need to reposition or adjust her.

3. Chasing the tail.

Once you've taught your dog to follow a piece of food and can control her movement, it is time to teach her to chase her tail. Initially, you want her to circle in one direction only. This will keep her from becoming confused and will allow her to become proficient at it. Pick either clockwise or counterclockwise, then stick with it. You can try the movement without the dog first to see which direction is easier and more natural for you to do.

Both you and your dog should remain standing throughout the training for this component. Initially, lean over her and utilize the food-leading technique to entice her into turning completely around by leading her in a large circle with your hand. Reward her with the treat and praise her by saying, *"Good."* It is helpful to introduce a verbal command, too. Later it will help communicate the trick to her at farther distances and assist you in the event she gets confused in a performance. I prefer the command *tail* for its simplicity, but I usually say, *"Get your tail"* so that it makes more sense to the audience. Repeat the process of having your dog turn completely around for a treat until she shows the slightest sign of boredom. Then move on to other training or go play with her.

Over several sessions, you have two goals to strive for in the training. Make whatever progress you can toward both goals in each session.

The first goal is getting your dog to turn around in a circle several times. Having her chase her tail for three or more rotations will be very impressive to your audience. The key to this training is to wait until she is great at turning around one time. You can then require her to do it twice before she gets her treat. Likewise, once she is great at turning around twice, require her to circle three times for the treat. You will find that as she circles each time she will look back to you briefly for the treat. At that instant, repeat the verbal command and give her a hand signal to keep going for another rotation.

The second goal is making a slow progression from the large movement of food leading to a small circular hand signal on a horizontal plane just above her head. After many repetitions, move this hand signal from being done directly overhead to being done farther and farther away. Eventually you should be able to give the hand signal from ten feet away.

Grab a kernel of food with your fingertips.

4. Reversing direction.

When your dog is terrific at chasing her tail in one direction, it is time to make her aware that she also has reverse available in her transmission!

Mitzi, a one-year-old long-haired dachshund, is learning food leading.

Use the same techniques you used to teach her to go in the one direction. The only difference will be the direction of your hand signal. As in most of your training, start out close to her with an exaggerated hand signal and progress to a smaller hand signal that you can give at greater distances. As she improves, get her to circle several times in each direction.

Final Thoughts

Once your dog is chasing her tail in both directions, practice them together as one routine. She'll be more dependable if you require her to do the same combination with each performance. I'd suggest having her chase her tail in her favorite direction for three rotations, and then switch directions for two more rotations before receiving the treat. To impress your audience with your control, tell her *"Reverse"* as you make the change to the opposite direction. This verbal command and the changing direction of your hand signal will alert her. She'll quickly learn the routine expected of her. Your only problem now is that you may have to start hiding the family car keys. After all, you've succeeded in creating a serious tailgater!

When you have taught this trick, you will have a head start in teaching the tricks found in Chapters 2, 9, 10, 11, 15, 17, 20, 22, 23, 24, and 25.

Lean over your dog.

Entice her into following the treat.

Tempt her into turning completely around...

...by leading her in a large circle with your hand.

Chapter 14

Having a Ball
Retrieving a ball too large to grab.

In this trick your dog will retrieve a large ball using his muzzle and paws to guide it. It's a fun trick to watch because he will have to make many decisions to figure out how to get the ball back to you and complete the task. When he accidentally sends the ball in the wrong direction, your audience will laugh and delight in his recovery. Realizing how hard it must be, they will be rooting for him and cheering as he gets the ball to you. Even if he performs it poorly by his standards, the audience will put him on the honor roll!

You should use a ball that is too large for your dog to grab. When he tries to grab it, you want the attempt to fail. He should be focused on just pushing and pawing it. Often, adding a little air to the ball will keep him from grabbing it and possibly puncturing it with his teeth. If you need to purchase a ball for the training, a colorful soccer ball makes a good prop. Once he learns the trick, you will want to experiment with balls of different sizes and weights. If he is overly enthusiastic and a bit out of control, a heavier ball might curb him. If he is a small dog, a very large but light ball might prove humorous. Selecting just the right ball will enhance the trick.

The training for this trick should be done both inside your home and outdoors on the lawn. Each will have advantages over the other. Indoors, the walls of a room provide borders to keep the ball in play and can be used as a training aid to help your dog guide the ball to you. Outdoor training is nice for teaching him to move around the ball in a herding fashion. There also are no coffee tables to get in the way!

In addition to your regular training sessions for this trick, have your dog do the trick to earn his dinner each day. If you'll excuse me for saying this, have him do a "dinner roll." His desire for dinner is a terrific motivator that will help speed the trick along to perfection. Let him watch as you prepare his food, have him perform the trick at whatever level he's at in the training, and then release him to eat his dinner as his reward.

There are two behavior components in this trick:

1. Pushing the ball.
2. Retrieving the ball.

Your dog needs to be proficient at the first before you proceed to the second.

1. Pushing the ball.

To teach your dog to push the ball, first encourage him just to touch it. Rub an enticing odor on the ball, such as a piece of hot dog or roast beef. Position yourself right next to the ball and say your dog's name followed by the command *"Come, nose it."* As he approaches, hold a little piece of the selected meat against the surface and allow him to grab it. Repeat this exercise until your dog moves quickly over to the ball to get the treat.

Now, duplicate everything again, but this time have your fingers positioned on the ball's surface without the meat. When your dog comes to grab it and makes nose contact with your fingers, praise and reward him with a treat using your other hand. As soon as he does this consistently, remove your empty fingers from the surface and, if necessary, tap the ball with your finger to encourage him to touch it. Over several training sessions, teach him to expect a treat every time he runs up and touches the ball with his nose. If you have a regression in the training, back up and repeat the previous steps.

As you progress in training your dog to push the ball, it becomes more important that he runs up to it to touch it. This can be accomplished by placing him in a *sit* before you give the command *"Come, nose it."* As your dog runs toward the ball to touch it, his momentum at contact will move the ball slightly. You want to encourage him verbally when he nudges the ball. Make a big deal out of it and get him excited. You can also very gently help his muzzle to move it and, of course, give him a treat. The key from this point on is to reward him with a treat each time he pushes the ball acceptably. Base this on the distance he's nudged it in his previous attempts. Help him, if necessary, so that he succeeds each time and earns the reward.

Once he is pushing the ball on his own, move away from the ball a few feet and practice again. Have him next to you and facing the ball. Say the command *"Go, nose it"* as you swing out your arm in the ball's direction. Gradually increase the distance you send him over several training sessions.

2. Retrieving the ball.

Once your dog is pushing the ball on command, you need to teach him to push it to you. This can be taught most easily by working in a hallway with all the room doors closed. The walls will help funnel the ball to you and make it easier for the dog. Start close to your dog and facing him. Put the ball between you and say his name followed by either *"Come, nose it"* or *"Come, bring it."* The command *bring* directs him to return immediately to you with the item. When he does and you grab the ball, quickly reward him with a treat. As

Cappuccine C.D.X., a five-year-old cocker spaniel, retrieves a ball that's too large for her to grab.

you grab the ball, slap it with both hands so that a loud noise is produced. This will act as positive feedback for him and he will learn that a treat is forthcoming. Repeat this process many times, backing up a foot with each successful attempt.

As soon as he is pushing the ball down the hall to you, it is time to start sending him for it. Take him to one

end of the hall. If one end has a doorway or steps that can't be closed off, go to that end. Roll the ball down the hall a few feet and send him to get it with the command *"Go, get it."* As soon as he gets to it, command him to *"Come, nose it"* or *"Come, bring it."* Be prepared to slap the ball when you catch it and then reward him. If he is not responding to your com-

Left: Use a hallway to teach your dog how to handle the ball.
Right: The walls will help funnel the ball to you and make it easier for your dog to learn.

mands, go back and review the previous training. If he did it with ease, roll the ball out farther the next time. Continue to practice until you can roll it all the way down the hall and he can bring it back.

Once your dog is good at rolling the ball back, add an obstacle that he will have to get the ball around. This will advance his abilities. Use an article that is soft and unbreakable, like the cushion of a chair. Place it so that it is slightly in his way. You want to present a situation that teaches him to roll the ball around any barrier. Add more items as he gets better. You'll notice that a lot of what he's learning is self-taught. He has a lot to figure out.

The last step is to practice the trick in different rooms and locations. Your dog will learn quickly as he encounters different situations.

Final Thoughts

Generally, I like to keep my need for props at a minimum, but this trick lends itself to an additional one. Since you have taught your dog to push the ball to you, you can dress up the trick further by merely adding a box for him to aim at. If you are handy, make a little soccer net. Just position yourself behind the item you want him to aim for, and give him the command *"Come, bring it."* He'll score big!

When you have taught this trick, you will have a head start in teaching the tricks found in Chapters 7, 16, and 22.

Zephyr, a ten-month-old soft-coated wheaten terrier, performs the stationary figure-eight pattern.

Left: Your dog begins in a heel position.
Center, left: On command, she runs through your legs...
Center, right: ...circles your right leg, and heads back through again.
Right: As she is circling your left leg, prepare to take a step with your right foot.

The moving figure-eight pattern.
Left: Your dog should walk through your legs, circling your right leg.
Left, center: Next, take a step with your left leg.
Right, center: As soon as she comes through your legs, bring your right foot forward.
Right: End the trick with your dog in the heel position.

Chapter 15

That Figures!

Performing a figure-eight heel.

In this amusing trick your dog starts out in a typical heeling position, but on command she will run through your legs in a figure-eight pattern, using your legs as posts to be circled. After she's been through your legs several times, to the audience's delight, you will start walking slowly. She will continue her pattern until you stop, at which time she'll return to the heeling position. The trick will be a hit because they've never seen a dog heel in such an odd fashion before and because most will assume they saw the complete trick while you were stationary. When both of you move at once, it's an unexpected delight. Although it appears to be a series of movements you need to teach your dog, it's really only one. You can count on her to figure it out!

Although this trick does not require that you teach your dog how to heel, it would be wonderful to demonstrate a heeling pattern before doing the trick. A dog that knows how to heel wins respect in the community and is able to go almost anywhere. People will love your dog because they see so few that are so well behaved and under control. A mugger would think twice before approaching a lady with

a well-trained dog heeling at her side. If you train your dog to heel, you will take her out more often and go more places. Your life and your dog's life will be enriched because of it.

If you are serious about teaching your dog to heel, I would suggest that you seek professional help. Obedience-training classes cover heeling, staying, jumping, retrieving, sitting, and lying down. For training purposes, the classes present many advantages. You will have the guidance of a professional trainer, your commitment will force you to take your dog out at least once a week, and in the classes your dog will have distractions to get accustomed to that she doesn't usually encounter at home. The distractions usually consist of other people and other dogs. You can be sure that when your dog learns in spite of all the distractions, she will be able to carry out your commands when you and she come home. You, your teacher, and the people you meet in the classes all have an interest in common—a love of dogs.

In teaching and performing this trick, you must be aware of the surface you are standing on. Your dog will have to make sharp turns and move quickly to make the trick look impressive. Good traction is a must! Carpet, grass, or any surface that provides good footing will work well. Avoid slippery surfaces like linoleum and hardwood floors.

There are five behavior components in this trick:

1. Food leading.
2. The *sit* position.
3. Assuming the *heel* position.
4. Learning the stationary figure-eight pattern.
5. Learning the moving figure-eight pattern.

It is important that you teach your dog the first and second components before trying to teach the others. Then you can proceed to work on the last three components. They should be taught independently. When you've completed a short training lesson on one, you can start the training of the next in the same session.

1. Food leading.

Please refer to Chapter 13, pages 74–75, for the training for this behavior component.

2. The *sit* position.

Please refer to Chapter 6, pages 39–41, for the training for this behavior component.

3. Assuming the *heel* position.

While you are standing in place, your dog should approach you and assume the *heel* position. She should sit straight on your left side facing the same direction as you are. As you will see, this works well as the starting and ending position during the performance of the trick.

To teach your dog to assume the *heel* position, grab some tasty treats and utilize the food-leading techniques you learned earlier. Give her the *heel* command, and tempt her into traveling up beside your left side. Initially, face the same direction as she is. This makes it easier for her, as she will not need to turn around. A little movement forward on your part will help draw her into position. Move forward, but only to the point where you can still coax her into walking up alongside you. If you hold a treat in your right hand and allow it to cross over to your left side, you'll have your left hand free to help guide her once she comes into range. As she approaches your left side, hold the treat in your right hand above her head and tell her to *"Sit."* If necessary, gently push down on her less attractive end and reward her with the treat. Release her with *"Okay"* and praise her with *"Good."* Repeat this exercise many times. It won't take her long to understand that she needs to position herself on your left side in a *sit* position to receive the treat. If you find that your pet has dif-

Tempt your dog to move up next to your left side.

Give the command sit *as you gently guide her into the* sit *position.*

Reward her with a treat.

ficulty sitting straight, try practicing next to a wall.

Once she is assuming the *heel* position with ease, it's time to make it a little harder for her. There are numerous things you need to practice independently until she masters them. First, instead of facing in the same direction as your dog, try facing in various directions before giving her the *heel* command. You will find the combinations that cause her the most trouble. She will need to teach herself how to maneuver to end up on your side in the proper position. Next, practice the exercise in a stationary position. This makes her rely solely on herself to make all the necessary adjustments.

As you progress, reduce the amount of coaxing needed, until all you have to do is give the *heel* command. And of course, be sure that you reward her with a treat.

The hand signal for the *heel* command can be very useful. It consists in patting your left side twice with your left hand. Use it as you give the verbal command *"Heel,"* and as your dog approaches your left side. The hand signal is also helpful when you want her to adjust her position slightly because she's too far back or at an angle. It will serve as a warning that she is not in the correct position and give her a chance to adjust. Later, in the course of teaching this trick, we'll use it to signal her that she has completed her figure-eight pattern and that she should return to the heeling position.

Training for the stationary figure-eight.
Left: Lead your dog through your legs with your right hand.
Right: Continue leading her to your front side.

Left: Your left hand should be ready to lead her back through your legs again.
Right: Ask a little more from her each time before offering a reward.

4. Learning the stationary figure-eight pattern.

To teach your dog how to run through your legs in a figure-eight pattern, stand and assume a little wider stance than you normally would. This will allow your dog a little additional room to work with. Place her in a *heel* position and utilize the food-leading techniques you learned earlier. Have a treat in your right hand. Start off each time by giving her the hand signal for the trick. The hand signal is done using your left hand and arm. It is best described as the action of a moving snake or the motion of waves on a lake. It's not important that you exactly duplicate the hand signal described. Whatever you do, it is sure to be unique from her perspective. Just be consistent in using the same hand signal each time. As soon as you finish giving the hand signal, give the verbal command *"Do it!"* This is a handy command that tells her to begin whatever you previously commanded her to do. As you give the command, reach your right hand around behind your right leg and present the food-leading hand signal between your legs. Tempt her to come through your legs to receive her treat. As she does, communicate that the trick is over by saying, *"Okay."* Repeat this many times until she has mastered it.

The next step in the training is to teach your dog to circle your right leg and come back through your legs again. You will be using both hands to food lead in this training, so have a treat in each one. Again, start off with your dog in the *heel* position and repeat the hand signal followed by *"Do it!"* As you've practiced, lead her through your legs with your right hand. Instead of giving her a treat and releasing her, continue leading her with your right hand until she is in front of you. Your left hand should be there with a treat to reward her. This will teach her to circle your right leg and look for your left hand. Make sure that each time you give her a treat, you preface it with the *Okay* command. After several repetitions, the left hand should be moved to encourage her to go back through your legs. To do this, reach your left hand around behind your left leg and present the food-leading hand signal between your legs. If you have proceeded slowly enough with the training, she should circle your right leg and find her reward. Repeat several times, using your left hand to lead her back through your legs before giving her the treat.

Continue the training for the figure-eight by asking a little more out of your dog each time before rewarding her. You want to keep leading her around until she sees the other hand to follow. With practice she should keep following the food-leading hand signals until you decide to give her a treat. For performance purposes she should complete two full figure-eights. This would equate to four passes through your legs. If you are having trouble getting her to make the switch from following one hand signal to the other, use only one treat and keep transferring it between your hands as you lead her.

5. Learning the moving figure-eight pattern.

You will be applying the same techniques as in the previous component to teach your dog the moving figure-eight pattern. The main difference is that instead of being stationary, you will start a slow walk. Hold a treat in your right hand. Place your dog in the *heel* position and give her the hand signal for the trick. As soon as you finish giving the hand signal, give the verbal command *"Do it!"* As you give the command, take one step forward with your right foot and present the food-leading hand signal between your legs. As before, do this by reaching your right hand around behind your right leg. Tempt her to come through your legs to receive her treat. As she does, communicate to her that the trick is over by saying *"Okay."* Repeat this many times until she masters it.

The next step is to teach her to circle your right leg. You will take a step with the left leg and tempt her to come back through your legs again.

As in the earlier training for the stationary figure-eight, you will be using both hands to food lead, so have a treat in each one. Again, start off with your dog in the *heel* position and repeat the hand signal followed by *"Do it!"* As you've practiced, step out with your right leg and lead her through your legs with your right hand. Instead of giving her a treat and releasing her, continue leading her to your front side with your right hand. Your left hand should be there with a treat to reward her. This will teach her to circle your right leg and look for your left hand. After several repetitions, take a step with your left leg just as she is circling your right leg. Use your left hand to encourage her to go back through your legs. To do this, present the food-leading hand signal between your legs by reaching your left hand around behind your left leg. If you have proceeded slow enough with the training, she should circle your right leg and find her reward. Repeat several times, using your left hand to lead her back through your legs to get a reward.

Continue the training for the moving figure-eight by asking a little more from your dog each time before you reward her. You want to keep leading her around until she sees the other hand to follow. Every time she circles a leg, you should take an additional step. With practice she should keep following the food-leading signals until you decide to give her a treat. For performance purposes, she should complete two full figure-eights—in

Training for the moving figure-eight involves the same procedure used for the stationary pattern; now, however, you tempt your dog to come through your legs while you are walking.

other words, four passes through your legs and four steps forward.

Once your dog has mastered this, it is time to teach her the ending of the trick. You want her to return to the heeling position each time before you reward her. The training for this and the corresponding hand signal were covered earlier in this chapter. Practice giving the hand signal just as she is coming through your legs from your right side. This will allow her time to slow down and come to a halt at your left side. As she does, make sure you bring your right foot up so that your feet are together. You both will look well heeled!

Combining the Steps

When your dog has mastered each of the behavior components, combine the trick as a unit and practice. Have your dog start in a *heel* position and run through your legs in a figure-eight pattern. As she completes her second figure-eight, start walking slowly. She should continue her pattern for another two figure-eights and then come to a stop at your left side in the *heel* position in order to receive her treat. My instructions on the number of figure-eights to do are merely

suggestions. It might be better to shorten the trick for a dog that maneuvers slowly through the routine. Likewise you might lengthen the trick if your dog is great at it and loves doing it. To help your dog look her sharpest, be consistent with what you request of her during a performance.

Final Thoughts

To advance the trick further, practice it in different locations and on dif-ferent surfaces. If you find the traction unacceptable on a particular surface, avoid ever demonstrating the trick on that type of surface. Don't slip-up and allow your dog to slip. Replacement parts are hard to come by!

When you have taught this trick, you will have a head start in teaching the tricks found in Chapters 4, 6, 9, 11, 13, 17, 21, and 23.

Chapter 16

Waste Management
Dropping trash in a flip-top trash can.

In this trick your dog will travel over and flip open the top of the kitchen trash can. He will then pick up a piece of trash off the floor, deposit it into the trash can, and complete the trick by flipping the lid closed. Your audience will be envious. You'll have a housekeeper that works for dog biscuits!

In the introduction of this book, I mentioned that it wouldn't be necessary to purchase props since the ones you will use are commonly found in the home. Although the flip-top trash can used in this trick is a popular style, some of you may have to purchase one.

A suitable trash can should be short enough for your dog to drop trash into from a standing position. There are shorter styles with flip-top lids available. Look for one whose lid extends over the edge of the can so that your dog has a nice lip to push.

You will want to stabilize the trash can for training and demonstrations by putting a weight in the bottom of it. Several books work well.

There are four behavior components in this trick:

1. Pushing the lid open.
2. Retrieving an item.

3. Dropping an item in the trash.
4. Flipping the lid closed.

Each component should initially be taught independently. Once you've completed a short training lesson on one, you can start the training of the next in the same session.

1. Pushing the lid open.

To teach your dog to push the flip-top lid open, first encourage him to touch the lip of the lid. Rub his favorite meat snack on the underside of the lip. The odor will encourage him to touch it. Instead of scenting the entire length of the lip, just do the middle few inches. This will make it easier for your dog to flip the lid. Position yourself next to the trash can and say your dog's name followed by the command *"Come, nose it."* As he approaches, hold a little piece of the selected meat in the scented area and allow him to grab it. Repeat this exercise until your dog moves quickly over to the trash to get the treat.

Now, duplicate everything again, but this time have your fingers positioned on the lip of the lid without the meat. When your dog comes up to grab it and makes nose contact with your fingers, praise and (using your other hand) reward him with a treat. As soon as your dog is consistent in doing this, remove your empty fingers from the lip and repeat the command *"Come, nose it."* If necessary, tap the top of the lid directly over the lip with your fingernail to encourage your dog into touching it. Over several training sessions, teach your dog to expect a treat every time he runs up and touches the lip of the lid with his nose. If you have a regression in the training, back up and repeat the previous steps.

As you progress in training your dog to push the flip-top lid open, it becomes more important that he runs up perpendicular to the long side or lipped edge of the lid. This can be accomplished by placing him in a *sit* position several feet from the trash can before you give the command *"Come, nose it."* As your dog runs toward the trash can to touch it, his momentum will nudge the lid up slightly. Encourage him verbally when he nudges the lip of the lid. Make a big deal out of it and get him excited. You can also gently hold his muzzle and help him to nudge it. Of course, reward him with a treat. The key from this point on is to reward him with a treat every time he pushes the lid up acceptably. Base this on how far he's nudged it open in previous attempts. If necessary, help your dog to succeed and earn the reward.

Once he is opening up the lid on his own, move a few feet away from the trash can and see if he can push the lid open. Have your dog next to you and facing the trash can. Say the command *"Go, nose it"* as you swing out your arm toward it. Over several training sessions gradually increase the distance you send him.

2. Retrieving an item.

The preliminary training for the retrieve is covered in Chapter 18, page 106. Once the retrieve is mastered using your dog's toy, practice the retrieve with a variety of easily held items. To jazz up the trick, you'll want her to retrieve an item that your audience will appreciate being thrown away. Consider using items such as an empty dog cookie box, the packaging from a diet dinner, or even junk mail that was addressed to your dog. You might even change the item depending on your crowd. For example, if you are entertaining friends at work, let your dog dispose of a competitor's product.

3. Dropping an item in the trash.

The preliminary training for the *drop* is covered in Chapter 12, pages 71–73. Once your dog has mastered the *drop* command, it's time to teach him the *"go, drop it"* command. You will also want him to start dropping a variety of items, instead of that uncomfortable one, for the remaining training. It is best to practice in a large, empty room that is free from all distractions. Select a large receptacle to catch the article to be dropped. An empty box in an unobstructed corner would be fine. The corner will direct his attention to the box you've placed in it and also control his path of travel between you and the corner. To make the *drop* easy for your dog, the box needs to be about four inches lower than your dog's mouth when he is standing. If necessary, cut off the top few inches of the box.

Have your dog *sit* about one foot in front of the box and *hold* the article. Say your dog's name to get his attention and follow this with the command *"Go, drop it."* The command *go* helps your dog understand that you want him to move away from you. If he doesn't move, ease him into a *stand* position while you support his jaw, with the article in it, from below. Allow the article to drop when his mouth is over the box. Reward your dog with a treat and a lot of praise. Over several training sessions, practice with the box until he is proficient at farther distances and in different locations. The key is to go slow and build up his confidence by allowing him to succeed. When he misses, command him to *"Get it"* and *"Go, drop it."* He should be able to recover the item quickly and drop it successfully this time.

Now that your dog has learned the command *"Go, drop it,"* transfer his knowledge to the much smaller drop zone of the trash can. Make sure you leave the lid open. Take it slow, and keep everything positive.

4. Flipping the lid closed.

Teaching your dog to flip the lid closed will be easy after he has learned how to push it open. You will find that the open lid extends well over the edge of the trash can. This

Combining the steps

Once your dog's training has progressed well with each of the components of the trick, combine the training as a unit.

Get your dog to *nose* the lid open and give him a treat while praising him. Then, tell him to *"Get it."* Gently direct him toward the article and assist him if required. Once he has grabbed the article, give the command *"Go, drop it."* Reward him for the steps you've combined and tell him, *"Go, flip it."* Again, give him a treat when he has nosed it closed.

When your dog is fairly close to mastering all the different steps of the trick, require him to complete the entire combination of steps in order to get the food reward. Talk to him a lot through this stage. Tell him what to do and praise him as he completes each step. If he gets confused, stop him with *"No!"* and then repeat the desired command.

...he mastered this trick in ten days.

Final Thoughts

For performance purposes, the less you say, the better. Talk your dog through a step of the trick only if he's having trouble. Be prepared! Your guests will probably want to rent him. Make sure they know that he doesn't do windows!

When you have taught this trick, you will have a head start in teaching the tricks found in Chapters 1, 7, 12, 14, 18, and 22.

gives him a large target to nudge. Use the same techniques presented earlier in this chapter for pushing the lid open. The only change you should make in the training is to use the command *flip* instead of the command *nose*. Although the commands request the same action, the different word will give him a chance to recognize that you want him to close the lid as opposed to opening it. To avoid additional confusion, never have your dog practice opening the lid and then follow by having him close it. Keep them separated by the other requirements of the trick.

Chapter 17

Sympathy Vote
Limping as if injured.

This is a perfect trick for the finale of any demonstration. Your dog will act as if she has an injured leg and will limp. She'll start out sitting while holding the injured paw up, hobble awkwardly on three legs, and finish by sitting again—still continuing to elevate the injured paw. She may look lame, but this trick is anything but!

In the limp, it will benefit you to have your dog use her right paw. There are other tricks, like shaking hands, that will require her to use her right paw. Using it now will avoid confusion later and will also be beneficial in future training. Having her use her right paw will also be convenient if *you* are right-handed. Since you'll be facing her in the training, your free hand is on the same side as the paw she has to lift.

Before you teach this trick, grab some tasty treats and your dog's leash. She will need to have her collar on. Any collar will do. If her leash isn't at least six feet long, get a comparable length of light rope that can later be tied to the collar. Find an area for the training that is free from distractions, provides you with room to back up about ten feet, and is level.

There are five behavior components to this trick:

1. The *sit* position.
2. Lifting the paw.
3. Standing while keeping the paw lifted.
4. The limp.
5. Sitting while keeping the paw lifted.

You should teach your dog the components one at a time. Wait to proceed to the next step until the previous one is mastered. The only exception to this is that once you've reached component three, you'll find it helpful to practice component five at the same time. You'll save some time in the training by going from three to five in the same lesson.

1. The *sit* position.

Please refer to Chapter 6, pages 39–41, for the training for this behavior component.

2. Lifting the paw.

You will be using both a verbal command and a hand signal during

Sonja, a seven-year-old Aussie shepherd/cattle dog, limps as if injured.

the initial training. Each will give you control the other doesn't supply. The verbal command *lift the paw* will help later when your dog is not looking at you and needs coaching. The corresponding hand signal will be given throughout the trick as a constant reminder to keep the paw elevated. It will also help to focus her attention on you for future orders. The hand signal for lifting her paw is always done with your right hand. To do it, hold your forearm vertically in front of you with your palm facing the left side. Allow your hand to flop to the left. If you are doing it correctly, your wrist should now be bent with your palm facing the floor.

To teach your dog to lift her paw, have her *sit* and position yourself on the floor in front of her with some treats. Using both the verbal and hand signal command simultaneously, gently lift her right leg with your left hand. Release her, using the command *"Okay,"* and reward her with a treat. The hand signal should remain in position in front of her until you use the release word *okay.* Keep a treat in the fingertips of your right hand while doing the hand signal so that you can get the reward to her quickly when she is released. When you lift her leg, gently support it just above the elbow joint, allowing her paw to flop down. This is not only how she'll want to do it naturally, but it's also better looking to an audience.

You will need to repeat this process over and over, pausing slightly after giving the commands in order to give your dog a chance to lift her paw on her own. Make a big deal out of it the first few times she solos. If she's not catching on, instead of lifting the paw completely, just keep her right paw from remaining in contact with the floor. Gently brush it forward every time she attempts to set it down. She'll give up trying and will lift her paw to a comfortable position.

Once your dog is lifting her paw on command, make sure you practice both the verbal command and the hand signal separately so that each will work independently. Now, gradually increase the time she'll continue to lift her paw. During the trick, she'll keep her paw raised for as much as 30 seconds.

3. Standing while keeping the paw lifted.

In the *stand* position, your dog's body is parallel to the floor, with her weight distributed equally on all four legs. To teach your dog the *stand* command, have her assume the *sit* position, helping her if necessary, and give the command. Gently lift the less attractive end of your dog with a hand under her belly, positioning her in a *stand.* Reward her with a treat and repeat. In just a few short training lessons, you'll need only a few fingers under her belly to let her know what you want. Make a big fuss over her the first time she does a *stand* without help from you. As with all the training you've done, your excitement means everything to her.

Once your dog is standing on command, have her *sit* and *lift the paw*. Give her the command *"Stand"* while displaying the hand signal for her to keep her paw elevated. When she attempts to place her right paw on the ground say, *"No! Lift the paw"* as you gently brush her paw forward to keep her from placing her weight on it. As soon as she complies, release her with *"Okay"* and reward. Repeat this process until your help is no longer needed.

It's also a good drill to have her *stand* on all fours and then *lift the paw* for a treat. This may come in handy and save a performance if she begins to put her paw down. As mentioned earlier in this chapter, it would be beneficial to incorporate the training for behavior component five along with this. You'll save some time!

4. The limp.

To teach your dog to walk while keeping one paw elevated, have her *stand* and attach a leash or light rope to her collar. Allow the leash to dangle straight down from her collar. Lift her right paw up and loop the leash underneath to gently provide support, thus cradling her paw. Back up from her a few feet while holding the leash up with your left hand. This should also keep her paw elevated.

Your right hand should be giving the *lift* hand signal as you tell her to *"Come, lift."* Tempt her with a treat, if necessary, to get her to take one step toward you. If she succeeds, be sure to reward her. Through several training lessons, gradually lengthen the distance she'll travel on three legs before giving her the food reward.

As soon as your dog is limping well with the support you're providing, discontinue it, but leave the leash on for training. (The general rule in this book is to reduce support gradually instead of suddenly discontinuing it. In this trick the support cannot be withdrawn gradually. If you have trouble, all you can do is begin training this behavior component again.) Allow the leash to hang a few inches below the lifted paw and every time her paw touches the leash repeat the command, *"No, lift the paw."* The placement of the leash is crucial. It must be at an uncomfortable height for her to rest her weight on, yet provide a means of catching her paw if it drops toward the floor. Proceed, literally, one step at a time. Wait until she's terrific at taking one step toward you with the limp before you go for two steps!

Once your dog no longer needs the "training wheel" support of the leash, you should remove it. If there is any regression, return to using the leash. You now want to refine your control of the limp while making it look as good as possible so that she gains the audience's sympathy. She must look convincing. She needs to move

Left: Loop the leash underneath your dog's paw to provide gentle support.

slowly as she limps, as if she is injured and in pain. You need to direct her with hand signals so that your verbal commands don't detract from the performance. Now that your left hand is free, this will be simple. You'll be using your left hand to give the *stay* hand signal after each limping step. While you're giving the *stay* hand signal with your left hand, your right should still be giving the *lift* hand signal. The purpose of giving the *stay* hand signal is to slow her limp down and make it appear that she has to struggle to take another step. The *stay* hand signal is given with the hand open and the palm facing her. For use with this trick, the fingers are most comfortably pointed up. Initially, use the verbal *stay* command in conjunction with the *stay* hand signal. Later you'll be able to drop the verbal command. If she moves after you give the command, quickly put her back into the position she was in and

repeat the *stay* command. She should learn quickly to remain motionless until your next command.

To get your dog to take that next limping step, discontinue the *stay* hand signal with your left hand while bouncing the *lift* hand signal slightly upward with your right hand. Initially, you might have to command her to *"Come, lift the paw."* When she limps and as her left paw hits the ground, again put up your left hand with the *stay* hand signal. This process will allow you to control a single limp, a pause, another limp, a pause, etc. With a little practice she'll limp slowly and be in full control.

5. Sitting while keeping the paw lifted.

To teach your dog to *sit* while keeping the paw lifted, have her *stand* and *lift the paw.* Give her the command *"Sit, lift the paw"* while displaying the hand signal for her to keep her paw elevated. As she sits, if she attempts to place her right paw on the ground, verbally say, *"No, Lift the paw"* as you gently brush her paw forward to keep her from placing her weight on it. As soon as she complies, release her with *"Okay"* and reward her. Repeat this process until your help is no longer needed. You should also require her to keep the paw lifted for about ten seconds after she sits. Do this by gradually lengthening the time you require her to lift it before rewarding her.

Combining the Steps

As soon as your dog's training has progressed well with each of the components of the trick, combine the training as a unit. Initially, you'll want the leash attached and in service in case she tries to cheat. Get her to *sit* and *lift the paw.* Instead of telling her to *stand,* use the *come* and *lift* hand signals, and command her to *"Come, lift the paw."* As soon as she stands with her paw elevated, tell her *"Stay,"* and reward her quickly with a small treat. Make sure you provide support to the lifted paw so that it doesn't touch the ground. You also want to continue quickly with the rest of the trick before she tires. Have her limp a few feet and tell her to *"Sit, lift the paw."* Again, provide her with

The lift *hand signal.*

Using the stay *hand signal to slow down the limp.*

101

any support she needs and give her a treat as she finishes the trick.

When your dog is fairly close to mastering all the different steps of the trick, require her to complete the entire combination of steps in order to get her food reward. Talk to her a lot through this stage. Tell her what to do and praise her as she completes the steps. If you are having trouble with a particular step, spend your next training session on that step alone.

Once your dog is doing the trick as a unit, practice the trick without having the leash attached and gradually lengthen the distance of the limp. Ten feet is tremendously impressive! Also, strive to reduce the use of verbal commands, relying more on the hand signals you've taught her.

Final Thoughts

If your dog has picked this trick up quickly, take it a few steps further!

Look for an area that has two or three steps to practice on. Typically, you will find such a step-down at the front entrance of your home or heading into your garage. Teach her to limp up and down the steps. Forgive the pun, but use the same step-by-step procedure! Also, you can teach her to limp uphill and downhill. Once she has mastered it, make it a wilderness setting by placing several branches for her to limp over.

Your four-legged thespian will steal people's hearts whenever she performs the limp. Make sure she returns them to your guests before they leave! And, be sure to remind her where her daily ration of dog biscuits comes from!

When you have taught this trick, you will have a head start in teaching the tricks found in Chapters 2, 4, 6, 10, 13, 15, 19, 20, 21, 22, 24, and 25.

Chapter 18

The Nose Knows

Selecting an item by scent.

In this trick your dog will travel over to smell a group of items, detect which one has your odor on it, and return with it. With a nose that size (no offense intended!), teaching this trick is just a matter of telling him what you want him to do. Your dog has an extremely sensitive sense of smell. If you compare your abilities to his in this category, you scarcely smell at all! (Which probably accounts for why you have so many friends!)

Unfortunately, your poor sense of smell is also the major problem in teaching him this trick. You can't be sure what he's smelling when he seems confused. Of all the tricks in this book, this one is the most time consuming to teach. It's not the difficulty of what you have to teach, but the extended time required between training lessons to make amply sure that all scents from the training items are removed. The good news is that this provides you with a perfect opportunity to pick an additional trick in the book to work on at the same time!

Audiences will love this trick. Even though most people know that dogs possess a keen sense of smell, they may never have seen a demonstration of it. They may also incorrectly assume that only certain breeds possess this ability. All will be immensely impressed and further educated.

Modern science is still unsure about how much better an average dog's sense of smell is compared to that of an average human. I once read that a famous bloodhound could find a trail that was many hours old and, by following it for only 50 yards, could determine which direction the person was traveling! It took less than a minute for that person to have walked that trail originally. It impressed me that the dog could detect whether the smell was getting stronger or weaker in such a short distance. Even if these accounts were exaggerated, I am still in awe.

Before you teach your dog this trick, you will need to collect at least seven items from your house that can be retrieved easily by him. Choose items that you don't use in everyday life and won't miss. Also, select ones that you won't mind getting damaged. They will be retrieved often and spend a lot of time outside in the sun and rain. Avoid absorbent items like pot holders because they will take

Ch. Ariel C.D., a six-year-old English cocker spaniel, selects an item by scent.

Left: Dog is sent to locate the scented item.
Center, left: Sniffing each item in the group...
Center, right: ...he correctly selects the scented item and...
Right: ...delivers it back to his owner.

longer to loose their scent after each use. The back of your kitchen drawers is usually a good place to start your search. Items like an old spatula, a measuring cup, a plastic glass, a fly swatter, or a squirt gun will work well. The more items you find, the more training you'll be able to get in. You will also need one or more boxes, depending on how many items you use. It's convenient to have one box for every seven items. You'll use the boxes to store the items outside in the sun and to transport them. Select boxes that have short side walls so that the walls won't entirely shade the items. Fold in any top flaps to add support and get them out of the way. *Important:* Add to this collection a pair of tongs so that you can move an item without touching it.

Once you have collected everything, you must allow the collected items to sit outdoors to air. Make sure everyone in your household knows not to touch or breathe on the articles. The longer you let the articles air the better. Two days are acceptable, three days are very safe. Initially, you don't want even a very old smell to confuse your dog. If you have collected many items, alternate the boxes. This way you'll be able to use a different box each day.

There are four behavior components in this trick:

1. Accepting being blindfolded or covered up.
2. Retrieving an item.
3. Selecting an item by scent.
4. Delivering an item.

Your dog needs to be proficient at the second component before teaching the others.

1. Accepting being blindfolded or covered up.

It's easy to teach your dog to accept being blindfolded or having his head covered up. If you have any sewing abilities, make him a blindfold to give a professional air to the trick. Otherwise, grab something lightweight to cover his head. A light jacket is handy and works well. Avoid anything that permits him to peek through it or look around it. Your audience will think he is cheating. Also,

you need to cover his head with something that will permit him to breathe.

To begin, grab a supply of treats and place him in a comfortable position. Block his vision with whatever you are going to use, while you command him to *"Stay."* After a moment, reward him with a treat. Repeat over and over, gradually increasing the time that his eyes are covered. Progress until long *stays* are attained with his vision blocked. If he moves, put him quickly back in the original position and repeat the command *"Stay!"* He should learn quickly to remain motionless until you uncover his eyes so that he can get a treat. Once the training is perfected, you'll uncover his eyes so that he can retrieve the scented item. Expect some laughs through this step of the performance. If your audience doesn't even giggle, have your dog show them to the front door!

2. Retrieving an item.

Dogs vary greatly in their ability to learn to retrieve. Most dogs instinctively chase an article that is thrown, and many will grab it. For the dog that does, teaching the *get* command will involve only some additional control. The dog that presently isn't a good retriever still has the instinct and, unknowingly, gets daily practice grabbing and carrying toys around. Toss a piece of food his way and you'll see a beautiful retrieve! This fact makes it easy to teach your dog the *get* command.

The procedure for teaching your dog to retrieve an object will involve the use of his favorite toy and some tasty treats. It is essential that you get him in a playful mood. The training will be more effective if you get down on the floor with him. Using his toy, play with him and build up his interest in the toy. Drop the toy in front of him, and say his name in an enthusiastic voice followed by the command *"Get it."* Often tapping the floor next to the toy or wiggling the toy will help. Do not play tug-of-war with the toy or you may have trouble getting him to release it to you later. If he succeeds in grabbing it, praise him, quickly take it away from him, and reward him with

a treat. If he fails to grab it, go back to playing and try again. Use your own judgment as to when you should stop the lesson. Let your patience and his enthusiasm be your guide.

If your dog doesn't seem to be catching on at all, the only answer is to get sneaky. Rub some of the treat on the toy, play with it, and drop it again. This time when you drop the toy leave a treat on top of it and give the command *"Get it."* Point out the treat if necessary. When he reaches to grab it, place the toy, food and all, in his mouth. Quickly remove the toy while praising him and allow him to eat the treat. Condition him by doing this over and over. Then repeat the steps but omit the treat. This time your dog will move toward the toy to look for the food. When he gets close, help move the toy into his mouth. Praise him as you exchange the toy for a treat. Practice these initial steps until a high percentage of success is achieved. Soon he will grab the toy quickly and receive his reward.

Once the retrieve is mastered using your dog's toy, practice it using a variety of easily held items. Walk around your house and have him retrieve various things, rewarding him each time.

3. Selecting an item by scent.

Throughout this training you will have to remain aware of the little things that might throw off your dog's performance. These little things will become less important once he has mastered the trick, but for now you want him to breeze through the lessons. To reduce confusion, avoid washing your hands with a fragrant soap or wearing new perfume just before training. Since you shed thousands of smelly cells when you walk, be cautious even carrying the box filled with the articles! Stay downwind of them and try not to breathe on them. When you get to the location of your training, minimize your movement in the area in which you drop the items.

The area you select should be well thought out. Pick one that has had no recent traffic. If you live in a large house, shut off a certain room and open a window. If you choose to work outdoors, pick an area that is unlikely to have had any traffic. A corner of your front yard that probably lacks people smells may have had a neighborhood dog pass by recently. Try to pick an area lined with linoleum opposed to carpet, or a patch of cement opposed to the ground, which naturally has a lot of intriguing smells. You might find a seemingly perfect place on the wooden deck outside your bedroom, only to discover that a rabbit lives underneath it! You'll be able to judge whether you should relocate by how the training is going.

To begin the training, use your tongs to set out one item. Make sure you touch only the handles of the tongs. Use them to grasp and posi-

tion all unscented items. Use your hand when moving all scented items. Now, get your dog and his favorite toy. Have him in control. He should not be allowed to run around the training area. Have him *sit* or put him on a leash. An assistant might come in handy. Have your dog grab his toy to impart a fresh scent on it and place it about a foot away from the unscented item. Tell him *"Go, find it,"* and praise him as he picks up the toy. Reward him with a treat in exchange for the toy.

If he grabs the other article tell him *"No,"* and gently knock the article out of his mouth. It is crucial that you keep things very positive and fun. Any corrections should be very light. Since the article he touched is now scented, put it aside and use your tongs to put another out. It is a good idea to remember the particular spot of each item, so that it can be avoided in the rest of the day's training. Repeat the command and the training until he is flawless with this exercise. Over several lessons it is your job to increase slowly the number of items he has to select from. All should be unscented except for his toy. Whenever he makes a mistake, back up in the training process and make his selection easier by removing some of the items. Proceed slowly with the training and don't overwork him.

At the end of each lesson, both you and your dog should scent all the items by holding them. Then put them back in the box, and return the box to its home outside. This way they will all smell alike and be allowed to air equally.

Now that your dog is correctly selecting his toy from the other unscented items with consistency, it is time to remove that toy from the selection process. Start by setting out an unscented item. Next, scent one of the other items for him to find. Hand this item to him so that both your scent and his will be on it. Place the item about a foot away from the unscented item and command him to *"Go, find it."* As in the previous training, gradually increase the number of unscented items over several lessons to make the search a little longer. Notice that I didn't say to make it more difficult. If you are proceeding as slowly as you should be, selection should not be difficult for him at all. Gauge your introduction of additional items by his success at picking out the scented one. You want to avoid the possibility of his ever failing.

Once your dog is able to find the scented item easily, it is your option as to whether or not you want to teach him to find the item scented by you alone, as opposed to one scented with both your scents. You can leave his training at this level and do the trick with ease. Just make sure you have him lick your hand so that you'll be able to impart his scent to the item later. I'd suggest you have him lick your hand immediately before the performance, out of your audience's view. Before you scent the item in question, blow a hot, moist breath into your hand to rekindle ev-

erything. If you want to continue the training so that he is able to find your odor among several unscented items, it is just a little bit more work. Begin with one scented item out of two, one out of three, one out of four, etc.

4. Delivering an item.

To teach your dog to deliver an item to you, it is first necessary that you train your dog to hold an item. If he is already holding his favorite toy whenever you hand it to him, you'll only need to teach him the command words, some movement, and a little manners in delivering it to you. If your

In teaching the bring command, help support your dog's jaw from underneath as he approaches.

Quickly exchange the toy for a treat.

108

Gently guide your dog into a sit position before accepting the article.

dog hasn't learned to hold an item, delay this training until you've taught your dog the *get* command, as described in the retrieving component in this chapter.

Throughout this training you'll be using your dog's name to get his attention, followed by the command *"Come, bring it."* Since your dog's action is always toward you on the delivery, the *come* command helps him understand that you want him to move in your direction. *Bring* directs your dog to return immediately to you while carrying the article he's holding.

To teach your dog the *bring* command, have him *hold* or *get* his favorite toy and then give him the command *"Come, bring it."* Praise his first attempt as he starts moving to-

ward you, and quickly exchange the toy for a treat. Initially, whenever he comes up to you with the article in his mouth, he may want to drop it at your feet. To help him overcome this habit, give support under his jaw to keep him from dropping the article, then exchange the article for a treat. It won't take long for him to realize that he needs to hold on to it until you take it from him in order to receive a treat.

Repeat the delivery training at a very short distance until your dog performs flawlessly and is having fun. Over several training sessions, slowly increase the distance of the delivery. If your dog drops the article, you are probably increasing the distance too fast. When this happens you should run up to him, put the article back in his mouth, and repeat the command as you back up a bit. Encourage him to complete the assignment and get his reward.

Once your dog has learned the delivery, gently guide him into a *sit* position before you accept the article. This results in a very attractive delivery. Over several sessions, increase the time that you make him *hold* the article before rewarding him. Your dog should be able to *hold* the article for approximately thirty seconds. This training ensures that, under the excitement of a performance, he won't drop it before you have time to accept it. When the delivery is mastered using your dog's favorite toy, practice the delivery with a variety of easily held items.

Final Thoughts

There are many different ways that you can demonstrate this trick. Your audience doesn't even have to know that your dog is making his selection by smelling them. Most dogs appear to be looking at the items and not smelling them at all. You can use identical items that only differ in color or are numbered. Tell him to select a certain color or number. He'll look brilliant! Another idea is to request an item by name and have him retrieve it. A good example of this would be to have him find the banana in a bunch of plastic fruit. It will appear as though he knows each fruit by name.

If you intend to trick your audience with one of these ideas, you won't be able to use your tongs to place the items. Seeing the tongs, the audience would smell something rotten! Once your items are adequately aired, put them in a brown grocery sack, fold the top edge over, and staple it. When you want to use them in training or for a performance, dump them out without touching them.

Regardless of what you do with this trick, it is advantageous to allow a member of your audience to select and hand you the item for the demonstration. This gets them involved, keeps you from being suspected of cheating, and gives you a chance to scent the item. Return the item to the same spot it was removed from, and make sure you point this out to your audience.

This is one of the few tricks that I am glad to repeat. You don't want people to get the idea that your dog was just plain lucky or that you signaled him in some way. The trick will still be impressive the second time. Be prepared for someone to ask you why you are not returning the last item your dog retrieved to the group of items. Tell them that you want to show off his knowledge of the other items; and, besides, he wouldn't be doing the trick at all if he wasn't "picky"!

When you have taught this trick, you will have a head start in teaching the tricks found in Chapters 1, 7, 12, and 16.

Chapter 19

Pretty Please!

The beg.

This traditional trick is popular because any dog can learn it in just a few short training sessions. In this trick your dog will balance back on his haunches in a vertical position with his front paws in the air. He will be a successful beggar because he only asks for a little cheap applause.

There are two behavior components to this trick:

1. The *sit* position.
2. The *beg* position.

The *sit* is one of the major body positions a dog can assume. Your dog must start out sitting so that his haunches are in contact with the ground. In this position all he has to do is rear back on them to beg.

1. The *sit* position.

Please refer to Chapter 6, pages 39–41, for the training for this behavior component.

2. The *beg* position.

The *beg* position is most easily taught by having your dog *sit* in a corner of a room that is free from distractions. Have him facing out and entirely backed into the corner, with his tail touching the intersection of the walls. The walls of the corner will help support him when he attempts to balance on his haunches. During the training, position yourself on the floor directly in front of him. This will provide you with total control, and, having little else to look at, he will focus all his attention on you. Besides, he is left with only a very small escape route!

To teach your dog to *beg,* you will use some kernels of food or other tidbits to entice him into the *beg* position. Have him *sit* in the corner while you take a tidbit and hold it in the tips of your fingers. This way he can see the reward and look forward to earning it. The food should be shielded from your dog so that he can't grab it. He might think you are handing him a piece of food, so you need to be cautious during the initial training to avoid being nipped accidentally. Proceed slowly and be prepared to correct any assault he makes. Yell *"No!"* and lightly shake his neck as a correction if he's being too aggressive. Your dog will learn quickly that *you* control the food.

Major, a seven-month-old collie, demonstrates the beg.

floor. Never reward him for an attempt when his haunches have come off the floor and he stands on his back legs. It is important for him to understand that he must remain in contact down there. If necessary, use your free hand to help hold that end down. Having him positioned in the corner helps prevent this, too.

As he raises his front paws off the floor, you'll notice that he has poor balance initially. You can help this by teaching him to shift his weight back over his haunches. As he starts to raise up, move your hand with the treat more toward the corner and over his tail end. Because he is following the treat, he'll move his head back and have better balance. Constantly check that he's backed into the corner all the way. This way the

Throughout this training, look for any small progress. Hold a tidbit above your dog, and allow him to grab it. Repeat the process over and over, but each time try to get him to reach up a little farther for the tidbit. Progress slowly, but never lose ground by asking less of him. If you were making great progress and then suddenly you weren't, your lesson on the *beg* was probably too long. Try to leave the trick on a high note by encouraging him to do it once more and then go play with him.

When your dog has learned to raise his front paws off the floor to grab the tidbit, make sure that his haunches stay in contact with the

Initially, use a corner to provide support for your dog.

112

walls will supply the necessary support, and he won't have the uncomfortable feeling of falling over backward into the corner. This could frighten your pet and slow your progress with the tricks. He might appreciate a little support from you. As his front paws come off the floor, grab both of them with one hand, and help him to shift his weight back and balance himself. You can even use this same method to teach him to fold his paws in toward his body. It will help his balance and make the trick look better.

As you practice, start using the *beg* command to initiate the trick. It is convenient to start using a hand signal now, too. Hold the tidbit in your hand above your dog's head. With the forearm vertical, move your hand up and down in short strokes while giving him the verbal command *"Beg."* Make the upstroke faster than the downstroke. This works well as a hand signal and helps direct his eyes to a spot that will help him keep his balance. Also, before you reward him after each repetition, use the release command *okay.* With this you will be controlling the time when the *beg* is over, instead of allowing him to decide.

Once your dog is balancing well in the corner, back away a step and try the *beg* again. Increase the distance each time your dog does well and decrease the distance each time he doesn't. As soon as he maintains his balance without any help from you, call him out of the corner and practice the trick. Expect him to regress a little at this point. You might have to review the steps in the training. This transition depends upon how much your dog relied on that corner.

Practice the *beg* until he is able to hold it for approximately ten seconds. For performances, ten seconds will be sufficiently impressive. You'll find that longer begs are difficult for most dogs, and not at all necessary.

Final Thoughts

This trick is well liked by all, but you must realize that it is no show stopper. Because of this, avoid repeating it for your audience. It tends to lose its appeal. If someone missed it because he was out of the room, let him catch your next performance. Also, since it is not a knock-'em-dead trick, don't end a performance of several tricks with this one. Put the most impressive trick last and preface it by warning your audience that it is your last. People appreciate being warned, otherwise they tend to be disappointed when they find out that the show is over.

Now that your dog is a pro at begging, don't be surprised if you find him pushing his food bowl around the room!

When you have taught this trick, you will have a head start in teaching the tricks found in Chapters 4, 6, 15, 17, and 21.

Chapter 20
Bowl-Legged
Digging in an empty water bowl.

This trick trains your dog to dig in an empty water bowl. It is a perfect trick to include in a performance consisting of several tricks. It will not only add variety to your performance, but your audience will enjoy it because, even though they know that digging is a dog's natural ability, they will never have seen it done on command before! The trick also has the advantages of requiring only a very limited amount of space and a small, easy-to-carry prop. Using a bowl allows your dog to dig without damaging property or the landscape. However, if yours is a prim and prissy dog,

Rashii, an eleven-month-old Akita, really digs this trick!

she may be forced to shed some of her dignity for the applause! Actually, just like any young football player, she will love playing in a bowl game!

If your dog spends her free time doing archaeological digging in your back yard and you're worried that this trick may encourage her bad habit, don't worry. Teaching her this trick actually might help solve your problem. By teaching her to *dig* on command for a tasty treat, it makes her back yard habit less enjoyable since she doesn't receive a reward for it. In some cases, it will extinguish the problem completely. Practicing the trick occasionally may help to fulfill her desire to dig. You'll also find this new line of communication helpful in redirecting a digging problem to a more suitable and unseen area of your back yard. For instance, after teaching her this trick, the next time you catch her digging tell her *"No dig!"* and run her over to the designated area. By encouraging her to *dig* in that area she'll learn that it is the proper place for that most enjoyable activity.

Any dog bowl can be used in this trick, but you might want to purchase

a special one for training and performances. It is advantageous to use a different bowl for the trick than for feeding and watering your dog. Upon seeing the special bowl, she'll instantly be signaled that the trick is forthcoming. Upon seeing her regularly filled water bowl, she will know that it is for drinking, not digging. If you do purchase a special bowl, get a large, flat-bottom ceramic bowl if possible. The weight of the bowl will keep it fairly stationary during the trick and the ceramic won't be scratched up with use. There are some lighter bowls that have nonskid feet or edging that will work well, too.

There are three behavior components in this trick:

1. The *stand* position.
2. Digging on command.
3. Digging in a bowl.

The *stand* is one of the major body positions a dog can assume. It's important that your dog stays in this position throughout the entire trick. After you've completed a short train-

ing lesson on the *stand,* you can teach the second behavior component. Wait to proceed to the third component until the second is learned.

1. The *stand* position.

Please refer to Chapter 22, pages 124–125, for the training for this behavior component.

Left: Here a playground with a gravel surface was used for the initial dig training.

At this stage of the training, it's important to drop the reward into the bowl. You want your dog to stare into the bowl and dig until the treat appears.

2. Digging on command.

Dogs will vary greatly in the time required to teach them to *dig* on command. It's easy from the standpoint that all dogs know how to dig. The trick is getting your dog to do it so that you can link it to the command word *dig.* When you get to the point that she paws the ground once, you are home free! Then, it is only a matter of encouraging her to do it better the next time.

If your dog is a real digger and has an area that she's permitted to dig in, take her there, some tasty treats in hand. If you don't know of such a spot, try taking a trip to the beach. The sand will give her paws little resistance, making it easy for her to dig. Encourage her by pointing at the ground and getting her interested in a particular spot. You can also try burying her favorite toy or a dog biscuit for her to find. Make a game out of it! As her paws start to dig, tell her *"Dig"* and that she is *"Good."* Once the digging progresses for a few seconds, tell her *"Okay"* and reward her with a treat. After the treat is eaten, use the *dig* command again. Repeat the process over and over until she has mastered the command.

An effective hand signal for *dig* is done by using both your hands in a digging fashion. You'll find it most helpful in directing her attention to a particular spot. You'll also use it for the next step in training her to dig on command.

If you are having trouble getting her to *dig* at all, take her paw in hand and help her scratch the surface. Be sure to be very gentle and reward her for every scratch, initially, until she gets the idea.

3. Digging in a bowl.

Once your dog is digging on command, it is time to transfer the training to the dog bowl. It is ideal if you can warm her up by having her practice digging in the area you've been working in. Put the bowl down next to or in the hole she's been digging, and continue with the training. If it is inconvenient to practice there, give it a try at home. The training might go a little slower, but you shouldn't have much trouble. If you do, you can always return to the site where you taught her to *dig* for your initial lesson with the bowl.

To teach your dog to *dig* in the bowl, get down on the floor next to the bowl and have some tasty treats ready. Throw a treat into the bowl and allow your dog to eat it. Repeat this several times to get her interested in the bowl as the source of treats. It's very important that the treat is always dropped into the bowl and not handed to her in this trick. This will cause her to stare into the bowl and dig until the treat appears. Otherwise, she'll be half watching you expecting her reward at any moment. Now, have her place her front paws in the bowl and reward her with a treat for standing in it. She will be reluctant, so you will need to gently help her place her paws in the bowl. Use the *stand* command you learned earlier. As with all the training in this book, if you've gotten to this stage easily, continue on. If not, leave your training on a positive note and pick it up again in the next training session.

Once your dog is happy to *stand* with her front paws in the bowl, have her do it, give the *dig* command, and encourage her as you did previously. The hand signal will be very effective here. If she's not getting the idea, take her paw in hand and start to scratch the bowl's surface. Again, be very gentle and reward her with a treat for initial scratches until she gets the idea. As soon as she makes her first attempt, no matter how poor, make a big deal out of it! The key from this point on is to drop a treat into the bowl every time she digs acceptably. Base this on her previous digging attempts. Encourage her to get better and better. With a little practice, you won't have to ask her to *stand* in the bowl, she'll dive in digging!

Final Thoughts

As soon as your dog is digging for five to ten seconds on command, it is time to practice this trick in different locations and with a variety of distractions. Then you'll be ready to show it to an audience. You can expect this trick to bowl them over!

When you have taught this trick, you will have a head start in teaching the tricks found in Chapters 2, 10, 13, 17, 22, 24, and 25.

Chapter 21

Snack Happy
Flipping a biscuit off his nose to catch it.

This trick starts with your dog balancing a dog biscuit on his nose, awaiting your command. He then flips it up into the air to catch and eat it. Your audience will find his initial restraint impressive and the concept of balancing the biscuit humorous. Your dog will flip for it, too!

This is a fairly easy trick that your dog can learn in just a few sessions and master by the time the last dog biscuit in the box says, "Adios, amigo." Initially, though, expect a few strange looks from your dog. He'll wonder why you're putting food on

his nose when it should be going into his mouth. Even he knows that!

There are several types and sizes of dog biscuits available. I use a major brand sold in grocery stores. Look for a type that any audience will recognize as a dog biscuit. For the initial training pick a dog biscuit for small to medium dogs that has flat surfaces. This will make it easier for your dog to balance and catch it. The dog biscuit should provide a snack without filling up his tank. The ones I use are almost two inches long and less than an inch wide. They come in a variety

Calvin, a three-year-old Labrador retriever, rarely lets one get away.

of colors. I save the brighter colors for performances and use the others for everyday treats. Whichever you select, make sure your dog likes them, too!

There are four behavior components in this trick:

1. The *sit* position.
2. Catching kernels of dog food.
3. Balancing a dog biscuit on his nose.
4. Flipping a dog biscuit into the air.

Each component should initially be taught independently. Once you've completed several training lessons on each, you can start combining the training as a whole.

1. The *sit* position.

Please refer to Chapter 6, pages 39–41, for the training for this behavior component.

2. Catching kernels of dog food.

The word *catch* will tell your dog that you are going to throw something to him and that you want him to catch it. It does carry with it a certain trust that must never be broken. Ask him to catch only those items that are completely safe for him to catch. His eyesight limits his ability to discern whether you are tossing a rock or a piece of food. Build his trust by being as faithful to him as he is to you.

Dogs vary greatly in their natural ability to catch things, but all dogs can be trained to do better than they would without training. Training involves throwing small kernels of food to your dog. Get him to lie down about five feet away from you, and toss him a piece of food. Keep your tosses gentle, and initially aim at his mouth. When he succeeds in catching the food almost every time, angle your throws slightly to the side. Increase the challenge as he improves. Build his catching ability slowly, always allowing him to catch more than he misses by adjusting the difficulty of your throws. Say the command *"Catch!"* and make the toss. He will learn the word *catch* quickly because he will know that something enjoyable is coming his way—by air mail no less! If his attention is not on you when you want him to catch something, say his name first, followed by the word *"Catch."*

Once your dog has the *catch* mastered, place him in a *sit* position and drop pieces of dog biscuit down from directly above him. This puts him in the body and head position he'll need

Before releasing your dog's muzzle, give the command "Stay!" *along with the* stay *hand signal.*

when catching the flipped dog biscuit. This practice will help him learn to catch the biscuit when he flips it off his nose later on.

3. Balancing a dog biscuit on his nose.

Initially, grab several whole dog biscuits as well as an ample supply of broken pieces. It is an advantage for you to reward your dog with the same type of food that you're tempting him with. Since his nose is working overtime on the dog biscuit he is balancing, you want his reward to match it in smell. The smaller the pieces, the better. You want to proceed as quickly as possible but you don't want to reduce his motivation by filling him up.

As you proceed, you will discover the best spot for balancing the biscuit. On most dogs, this spot is located on the top of the muzzle where the hair meets the nose pad. Try this spot first. Later, with experimentation, you can locate the optimal location by moving the biscuit in either direction. Lay the dog biscuit *across* the nose, not lengthwise on the muzzle. This requires more balancing and gives the trick a polished look. Having the biscuit in this position will also help your dog be more consistent in launching the cookie since he has less area of contact with it.

To teach your dog to balance the biscuit, place an entire biscuit on his nose while holding his muzzle level and closed with your other hand. Before releasing his muzzle, give the command *"Stay!"* and the *stay* hand signal. This hand signal is performed with the hand open and the palm facing the dog. The fingers can be pointed to the side, down, or up. It should be given as close to his nose as possible and remain there until you tell him to flip the biscuit. Let go of his muzzle for just an instant, and grab it again to regain control. Quickly remove the dog biscuit and reward him with a broken piece. You want to repeat this process over and over, increasing the time he balances it. Make sure that if the biscuit is dropped he doesn't eat it. If he should, he would be rewarded for improper behavior.

Try to use the hand signal to control the levelness of his nose. If his nose gets tilted up, it will be impossible for him to flip the biscuit straight up in the air to catch it. He should stare at your open palm. You can help this by tapping your palm with a finger from your other hand. If you control his eyes, you control his muzzle. Over several training sessions, your job is to get him to be able to balance the dog biscuit with a level nose for approximately 20 seconds.

Once your dog is balancing the biscuit with ease at close range, start increasing your distance from him. Give the command *"stay"* and the hand signal, then scoot back slightly. Keep the hand signal at his nose level. With practice, you should be able to give the hand signal, walk back several feet, squat down facing him, and again use the hand signal to continue your control.

4. Flipping a dog biscuit into the air.

To teach your dog to flip a dog biscuit up into the air, you'll need to help him do it until he "catches" on. Place a dog biscuit on his nose as you hold his muzzle with your other hand. Loosen your grip so that you are merely supporting his jaw from below. Now, give the command *"Flip it"* and help him toss the dog biscuit straight up into the air. Immediately give the command *"Catch it."* You will want to reward him with a small piece of dog biscuit every time you go through this process until he makes his first few attempts at opening his mouth to catch the biscuit. Once this happens, cut back on rewarding him every time, thereby making it more worthwhile for him to catch the whole dog biscuit. If you are having trouble, be patient. You might find it helpful to spend more time on the second behavior component, which covers the training for catching items. Additionally, whenever you give the *flip* command from here on, change the *stay* hand signal into an upward flick of your fingers. This will further communicate your wishes.

As soon as your dog is catching the dog biscuits, it is time to encourage him to *flip* it on his own. Place a biscuit on his nose, give the command *"Flip it,"* but pause momentarily without helping him. He'll be excited, so give him a chance to try it on his own. When he does, he will probably miss the catch, so make sure you quickly encourage him by giving him a piece of dog biscuit. If he doesn't try to *flip* it, help him. It'll only be a matter of time until he solos!

Final Thoughts

Wait until your dog is catching the dog biscuit 50 percent of the time before you show this trick to an audience. During a performance, it's okay if he misses it a couple of times. If he misses it three or more times your audience will feel sorry for him, and you'll look like the bad guy. If he tends to flip the dog biscuit behind him, balance it more toward the end of his nose and make sure his muzzle is level or a little lower at the start. If he has found the training and trick easy from the start, try combining this trick with the *beg* (see Chapter 19, "The *beg* position," pages 111–113). Have him *beg* then balance the dog biscuit on his nose and give him the *flip* command.

I'd bet paws down that this trick will be your dog's favorite. It'll take some practice, but he'll love every biscuit of it!

When you have taught this trick, you will have a head start in teaching the tricks found in Chapters 4, 6, 8, 15, and 17.

Chapter 22
Shut Up!
Closing a door.

This trick converts your dog into an automatic door closer. You no longer need to visit your local supermarket to enjoy such a nice feature! Another nice thing about this trick is that, with a little training, your dog will be able to recognize even unfamiliar doors and close them when asked. Because of his ability to recognize certain objects, the word *door* will be introduced into his vocabulary.

Joshua, a three-year-old Newfoundland/German shepherd, closes a door.

This trick is much easier than it looks. A door appears to be a large chunk of wood. It has the reputation of being a barrier. Even the neighbors of Mr. Door are a rough sounding lot with names like Stop, Lock, Jam, Frame, and Threshold! The fact is, most doors around the house are real swingers—hollow swingers at that. They are made with thin sheets of ply over a hollow core. The door's weight is adequately supported on hinges and swings easily. Even if a door is solid wood, most dogs can push it, regardless of their size.

For the sake of your door, your dog will be required to push it closed with his muzzle. Never allow him to paw the door. His nails will scratch the door in question, as well as any other door in the house that he wants to get through. If he tries to paw the door closed, lightly slap his paw, tell him sternly that he's been *"Bad,"* and then get back to a positive note by returning to the training.

There are two behavior components in this trick:

1. The *stand* position.
2. Pushing a door closed.

The stand is one of the major body positions a dog can assume. It will make it easier for your dog to learn the trick if he remains in this position. After you've completed a short training lesson on it, you can proceed in teaching the second component as long as you are aware that he needs to remain in a *stand.*

Give the command to stand.

Gently help your dog into position.

Gradually lengthen the time he stays in the stand.

123

1. The *stand* position.

In the *stand* position, your dog's body is parallel to the floor, with his weight distributed equally on all four legs. To teach your dog the *stand* command, have him assume the *sit* position, helping him if necessary, and give the command. Gently lift the less attractive end of your dog with a hand under his belly, positioning him in a *stand*. Reward him with a treat and repeat. Once the *stand* command is given, he should remain in the *stand* position forever, theoretically, until he is released by you with the *okay* command. In just a few short training lessons, you will only need to place a few fingers under his belly to let him know what you want. Make a big fuss over him the first time that he does a *stand* without help from you. As with all the training you've done, your excitement means everything to him.

Throughout the training for this trick, whenever your dog leaves the *stand* position, repeat the command "Stand," help him into the position if necessary, and praise him before returning to the lesson. The *stand* position allows him the mobility to complete this assignment with ease.

2. Pushing a door closed.

To teach your dog to push a door closed, first encourage him to nose the door at the proper spot. Since most doors swing into a room, this spot is located on the room or interior side of the door, below the door knob, at about muzzle height. Position yourself right next to the door and say your dog's name followed by the command "Come, nose the door." As he approaches, hold a tasty treat in the area and allow him to grab it off the face of the door. Repeat this exercise until your dog moves quickly to the door to get the treat.

Now, repeat everything again, but this time have your fingers positioned on the door without the treat. When your dog comes up to grab it and makes nose contact with your fingers, praise and reward him with a treat using your other hand. As soon as your dog is consistent with this, remove your empty fingers from the door and, if necessary, tap the face of it with your fingernail to encourage your dog into touching it. Over several training sessions, teach your dog to expect a treat every time he runs up and touches the door with his nose. If there is a regression in his learning, back up and repeat the previous steps. If you are not seeing any progress, try gently to help his muzzle nudge the door and give him a treat. Repeat until he gets the idea. This can be an alternate way of teaching the trick.

There are two ways of approaching the rest of the training. Both should work well to master the trick, but try them both in case one works better. The first approach is to have your dog run up perpendicular to the door's face. This can be accomplished by having him in a *sit* position with the door nearly closed. Then give him the command *"Come, nose the door."* As your dog runs toward the door to touch it, his momentum will nudge the door slightly closed. The second approach is to have the door pushed back against the wall initially, then funnel him into this area behind the door. This effectively gets the door moving in the right direction. With either approach you want to encourage him verbally as he nudges the door and give him a treat. Make a big deal of it and get him excited.

The key from this point on is to reward him with a treat each time he pushes the door closed acceptably. Base this on the distance he's nudged it closed in previous attempts. Encourage and help your dog each time so that he succeeds and earns the reward. Try to get a little bit more out of him each training session. You'll find that the greater the distance he has to swing the door, the easier it will be for him to build up the momentum necessary to fully close the door. The door's latch should snap into place to end the trick.

Once your dog is pushing the door closed on his own, move away from the door a few feet and practice it again. Have your dog next to you and facing the door. Say the command *"Go, nose the door"* as you swing out your arm toward the door. Over several training sessions, increase the distance you send him.

Final Thoughts

Once your dog is proficient at one door, it is time to head around the house and practice with all of them. You'll find that each door will present its own challenge initially. Your dog might be confused about which way to push a particular door. He also might be thrown off by a panel door that has a multi-level surface. Doors to the outside will be heavier and will require him to work a little harder. Still others will have plants or furniture close enough to make him adjust his techniques slightly. Once each door in the house is mastered, you'll want to continue his education elsewhere.

When you have taught this trick, you will have a head start in teaching the tricks found in Chapters 2, 7, 10, 13, 14, 16, 17, 19, 20, 24, and 25.

Ch. Pippin, a two-year-old Bernese mountain dog…

...is now reaching
new heights in her
training!

Chapter 23
Higher Education
Climbing a ladder.

It is important that you end a performance of several tricks on a high point and warn your audience that it will be your final trick. This trick could easily provide you with such a climax. In this impressive trick your dog climbs a ladder. Your audience will appreciate the difficulty of this trick just by watching the painstaking procedure that your dog must go through. They'll love it!

This trick contains an element of danger that the other tricks in the book do not. Since your dog will be climbing, there is the possibility of her slipping and injuring herself. You need to weigh the risks, since each case will be different. A small dog might not have enough body length to climb a commercially made ladder safely. A large dog might be too bulky for you to catch safely if she slips. Some dogs might be too heavy to lift off the ladder at the end of the trick. Do not attempt to teach this trick unless both you and your dog are physically fit! Throughout the training and the performance of this trick you can minimize the danger by staying close to her. You are her safety net! Although I have never had a dog even slightly injured performing this trick, I did have an awful scare once. I had climbed an extension ladder to my roof and was doing some maintenance when I discovered I had company. Although it was nice to have an assistant to hand me tools, I now make sure my dogs are in the house whenever I get ready to do any work on my big ladder!

Almost any ladder will work for the training. A six-foot wooden stepladder is ideal to demonstrate the trick. It provides solid footing for your dog, is self-supporting, can be cheaply purchased, and is a handy size to have around the house to reach things! If you don't own such a ladder and are on a tight budget, you might be able to pick one up at a garage sale in your area. Another option is to train your dog at your local playground. The ladder on the slide is usually perfect. If you use a taller ladder, make sure your dog climbs only as high as you can safely lift her down. You will have to lift her down each time at the end of the trick.

There are two behavior components in this trick:

1. Food leading.
2. Climbing a ladder.

Wait until you have the first component mastered before moving on to the second.

1. Food leading.

Please refer to Chapter 13, pages 74–75, for the training for this behavior component.

2. Climbing a ladder.

Once you understand what a dog needs to do to get up a ladder, teaching her is easy. There are three movements she must make, then the movements are repeated over and over. First, she must place both of her paws up on the highest rung she

Left: Have your dog place both of her paws on the highest rung she can reach.
Right: Help her put her rear paws on the first rung while patting an upper rung to encourage her to climb.

Left: Tempt her head out from between the rungs with a treat.
Right: Repeat the process.

can reach when standing on her hind legs. Have your dog approach the ladder and encourage her by patting an upper rung while holding a treat in your hand. You can help her out by getting behind her and lifting her up. In these early attempts reward her with a treat each time she succeeds in moving her paws up onto the next appropriate rung, with or without your help.

Once in this position, the second movement requires her to lift her rear paws up on to the first rung of the ladder. To do this, encourage her by patting an upper rung while holding a treat in your hand. As you do this, use your other hand to lift a rear paw and help place it on the first rung. Once one paw is there, gently lift your dog's hindquarters and help the other rear paw find the same rung. Reward your dog with a treat for accomplishing this step, and continue on to the third movement.

The third movement is necessary because most dogs will push their weight up the ladder and end up with their heads positioned between its rungs. The object of this step is to get your dog to pull her head out from between the rungs and to look up the ladder. Use the food-leading techniques you've learned to tempt her head out from between the rungs and reward her with a treat. A gentle push on her head might be necessary until she gets the idea. If your dog is the exception and keeps a clear head, just skip this step!

Once your dog has completed the third movement, repeat the series again and again. Have her move her front paws up onto the next rung first. Then have her move her rear paws up onto their next rung. Finally, have her pull her head out from between the rungs so that she is ready to proceed up the ladder again. Start using the verbal command *go, up* from here on. Through all the early training, reward your dog with a treat and a lot of praise for accomplishing each required movement. Later, as she gets the hang of it, reward her only when she completes all three movements. Once she has mastered the trick, require her to climb all the way up the ladder to get her reward.

Final Thoughts

No one should be able to criticize your dog for having lofty pursuits. Even though it's a dog-eat-dog world out there, she was able to climb her way to the top!

When you have taught this trick, you will have a head start in teaching the tricks found in Chapters 9, 11, 13, and 15.

Chapter 24

Peek Performance

Peeking out from under a tablecloth.

A single command will have your dog delighting your audience by peeking out from his canine hideout. It's a silly trick that has your dog waiting under a table for your command. When given, he'll slowly walk out from under the draped tablecloth until his eyes are just barely uncovered. At this point, he'll freeze with the tablecloth still draped across the top of his head. It's a picture few forget! Not only is this trick easy to teach and a real crowd pleaser, but, in fact, it's all done under the table!

Tablecloths are made out of all sorts of fabric and other materials, like paper and plastic. They all work well for this trick. It's not a problem if the tablecloth is long, only if it is too short. The tablecloth you use must hang over the table far enough to be at least as low as his nose when he is standing. If you have a tablecloth that is a bit shy of these requirements, merely pull it down slightly on the side of the table that faces the audience. If you have a very small dog, you'll need an extremely large tablecloth that will drape low. Instead of investing in a floor-length tablecloth, practice the trick by taping a tablecloth or other material to the table so that it is at the proper height. Once your dog has the trick mastered, transfer the training to floor-length drapes in your home. Teach him to go behind the drapes and peek out from underneath them. You may have to live with hairy drapes, but the trick will be as cute as if you had used a tablecloth!

There are four behavior components in this trick:

1. The *stand* position.
2. Waiting under the table.
3. Walking slowly.
4. Peeking out from under a tablecloth.

The first three components should be taught independently. Once you've completed a short training lesson on one, you can start the training of the others in the same session. Wait until the first three are learned before proceeding to the fourth component.

1. The *stand* position.

Please refer to Chapter 22, pages 124–125, for the training for this behavior component.

Chester, a seven-year-old English springer spaniel, finds it hard to hide his talent.

Delay the training for the slow *command until you have the help of an assistant.*

The slow *hand signal is given with the hand in the* stay *position by closing the fingers into a fist.*

As you give the stay *hand signal, have your assistant give a gentle tug on the leash.*

With practice, your dog will learn to stop his forward movement on his own.

2. Waiting under the table.

During the training for this component, it is important that you have the tablecloth on the table. This will make the training easier because the tablecloth acts as a barrier for your dog. To get him in position to do the trick, either lead him over to the table or go to the table and call him to you. Lift an edge of the tablecloth and gently guide him under it. Once he is under, allow him to turn around and then give him a treat. This pulls him back to your side of the table so that you can maintain control and keep him from leaving. It also accustoms him to facing the right direction for performing the trick. Drop the tablecloth for a few seconds, lift it, and reward him with a treat. As you practice, gradually lengthen the amount of time he must be patient. Continue this until he is able to stay under the table for approximately one minute. He'll learn to do this quickly. If your pet persists in trying to escape, drape a sheet to the floor on the back and sides of the table. Once he gets the idea that he must wait under the table, phase out the sheet by gradually raising it.

I caution you to avoid using the *stay* command because you can't really see if he is, in fact, staying. Since you don't know when to make a correction, you could weaken the usefulness of the command. If you feel like you need to use a word command, use *wait*. The *wait* command is effec-

Once your dog has this trick mastered, you'll find it easy to transfer the training to floor-length drapes if you wish.

tive when you want your dog to stay in a certain area but don't mind if he moves around slightly for comfort or maybe a better view. I use it when I visit a friend's house. He is allergic to dogs, so I leave my four-legged companions on the front porch with the *wait* command. My dogs know that they can move around but cannot leave the porch. In the case of remaining under the table, the *wait* command allows your dog to walk around underneath but not to leave.

3. Walking slowly.

Please refer to Chapter 10, pages 60–61, for the training for this behavior component.

4. Peeking out from under a tablecloth.

Wait to teach this behavior component until after the others have been mastered. This component combines the other separate behaviors and utilizes the same training techniques. If you are having any difficulty with the training for this component, back up and review the particular area that's giving you trouble.

To teach your dog to peek out from under the tablecloth, place him under the table awaiting your command. Ini-

tially, position yourself on the floor in front of the table. This will add to your control. Use the *slow* command and as his head emerges wait for the tablecloth to pull slowly off his muzzle revealing his eyes. At this point, have the *stay* hand signal already displayed and require him to freeze in this position. With a little practice, he'll learn to hold the position without even a signal from you. You do need to release him from this position. During a performance, wait until the chuckles just begin subsiding and then release him with *"Okay"* and reward him with a treat.

Final Thoughts

Once your dog has this trick mastered, you can cue him into action by simply telling him to *peek*. Entertaining your audience with an elaborate story about the counterespionage surveillance techniques he learned overseas might "pique" some interest, too! You know that, no matter what, when he comes out from underneath the tablecloth, the outcome will be the same—the crowd will love him!

When you have taught this trick, you will have a head start in teaching the tricks found in Chapters 2, 10, 13, 17, 19, 20, 22, and 25.

Chapter 25

Bow-Wow!

Taking a bow.

The *bow* is another of the traditional tricks that all dogs are supposed to know. It will be the finale of your demonstration, an acknowledgment of your audience's applause. It is also your last chance to win the audience over! Performed well, it's a good trick, but not a heart stopper. Since animal trainers want to end with one of their flashier tricks, pick your most impressive trick and announce that it will be your last. After you perform it and while the crowd is still in a roar, slip in the *bow.* It's up to you whether you pointedly tell your dog to take a bow or just use the *bow* hand signal. The trick will be successful because you didn't use it as a feat of amazement, but as a touch of good manners.

Most dogs assume a bowing position naturally in play or during a stretch after a long rest. To make the *bow* a notable trick for your audience, you will teach your dog a few minor improvements. From a standing position, your dog will lower the front of her body, keeping her hindquarters elevated. As she assumes this position, she will leave both paws outstretched along the floor and lay her muzzle on them. Responding to your hand signal, she'll thank the crowd with a vocalization as she raises back up to the standing position.

The training will be easier if you construct a plywood stanchion that prevents your dog from lowering her hindquarters. Since it is only used for training purposes, it can be made from scrap materials. Ideally, it should be a few inches shorter than the distance between the floor and her belly when she is in a standing position. The measurements are not crucial; it just needs to prevent her from lying down. It is nice to have it approximately twice her width. This will prevent her from sidestepping around it to lie down. The plywood stanchion can be any thickness but it must be strong enough not to bend from her weight. Also, the stanchion should be self supporting. If you lack carpentry skills or a carpenter friend, you can use any heavy item that will support the plywood upright on both sides to make the stanchion.

There are five behavior components in this trick:

1. The *stand* position.
2. The *down* position.

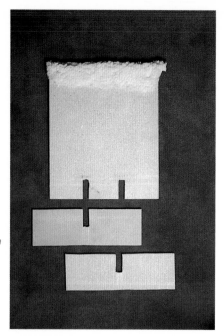

A serviceable design for a stanchion, which you can construct quite easily from particle board, plywood, or any available piece of scrap lumber.

3. The bow.
4. Resting her muzzle on her paws.
5. Talking.

The first two are helpful body positions that will aid you in the training process for the *bow*. Wait until these are learned before proceeding to teach the third component. The initial training for the last two components can begin at any time.

1. The *stand* position.

Please refer to Chapter 22, pages 124–125, for the training for this behavior component.

2. The *down* position.

Please refer to Chapter 9, page 56, for the training for this behavior component.

3. The bow.

To teach your dog the *bow,* have her *stand* along a wall and slip the plywood stanchion under her belly. The wall will prevent her from side-stepping the stanchion on one side. You control the other side. Show her a tasty treat and place it at her front paws. Hopefully she will assume the bowing position and pick up the treat.

As she is retrieving the treat, give the hand signal for *bow* along with the verbal command. The hand signal is done by opening both hands with your palms facing the ground. With your thumbs touching each other, move your hands away from you. After you give both of the *bow* commands, give the *down* command, too. This command will help her to understand your desires; it should be skipped as soon as she grasps the concept. If she doesn't naturally assume the *bow* position, give both the verbal command and the hand signal. Then, using one hand, gently slide her front paws out. The other hand should be placed toward her rear and slightly under her belly. This hand controls against her trying to sidestep the stanchion and provides a comforting scratch to her belly, reinforcing that everything is all right. Reward her with the treat as soon as she is in the *bow* position, praise her, and command her to *"Stand."* Repeat this many times over several sessions. Help her less and less, until

The bow *training. Left: A wall will prevent your dog from side-stepping the stanchion. Right: Place a treat at her front paws. You want her to assume the* bow *position to acquire the treat.*

Left: Help her if necessary by gently sliding her front paws out. Right: Reward her with the treat as soon as she is in the bow *position.*

137

she can assume the *bow* position on her own. As with all the training, keep everything positive and fun!

Once your dog is bowing without your help, it is time for her to try bowing without support from the stanchion. Start your training session off using the stanchion and have her do the *bow* several times. Now, remove the stanchion but continue to use your hand to provide that comforting scratch to her belly as you give her the *bow* command. Your hand can provide the necessary support until none is needed. As soon as this occurs, begin increasing the distance you're able to stand away from her while she performs the command.

4. Resting her muzzle on her paws.

To teach your dog to rest her muzzle on her paws, have her climb up into a soft chair or couch and lie down. If possible, control her front end so that her muzzle is near the front edge of the chair or couch. Position yourself on the floor directly in front of her. This difference in height will help direct her attention and her muzzle downward. Give her the verbal command *"Muzzle"* and use your index finger to point down. Keeping your hand signal visible, use your other hand to push her muzzle gently until it is resting on the front edge of the chair or couch. Release

her with *"Okay"* and reward her with a treat. Repeat the training until she responds well to both the verbal command and hand signal.

Once she has mastered the *muzzle* command while lying down on a piece of furniture, apply the same training techniques when she is lying on the floor. This will be more difficult since her tendency will be to look up at you. Make it a gradual change by starting the training lying on your stomach in front of her. As she continues to succeed in resting her muzzle on the floor or her paws, assume a slightly higher posture. With practice, you should eventually be able to stand as you give the *muzzle* command.

Throughout this training it is important that her muzzle assumes an attractive position. It is equally important that she is conditioned to go to this position early in the training so that time isn't wasted in retraining her later. Experiment with how her muzzle can rest on her paws. Once you've found your preference, gently help her muzzle into place each time before rewarding her. I prefer the dog's paws to be together with the muzzle resting slightly across and to the side. Another popular choice is having the dog's paws slightly separated, with the muzzle resting directly between them on the ground.

The remainder of the training for this behavior component should not be started until the *bow* training is well along. At that time you will combine the additional requirement of resting her muzzle on her paws with the *bow,* maintaining that position until the end of the trick. Gently help her comply, if necessary, and release and reward her with a treat. With repetition, she'll surprise you. She'll automatically put her muzzle down with the *bow.* You'll only need to use the *muzzle* verbal command and hand signal as occasional backup commands to keep her sharp.

5. Talking.

A talking dog has an enriched personality compared with one that doesn't talk. Your dog makes a variety of vocal sounds that can be utilized in your trick work. Each vocal expression can be taught to her and linked to a word associated with the vocal noise. The vocal expressions possible are *little woof, cry, moan, howl, bark,* and *growl.* For this trick, pick a pleasing sound that she already makes and uses. Then, teach her to do it on command.

To teach her to talk on command, strongly encourage her whenever she makes the sound that you are attempting to teach. Make a big fuss over her when she makes that particular noise. Once she is making it often, find an appropriate word to associate with it. In your training sessions, ask her to make the sound while tempting her with a piece of food. Often, mimicking the particular sound will help. If your dog is trying hard and moving her mouth but no

sound comes out, you might want to reward her efforts anyway. Have patience. It sometimes requires a lot of encouragement.

The easiest, but not the most pleasing, vocal expression that you can teach your dog is the *bark.* If you are having trouble teaching her another vocal sound, often teaching her the *bark* first will lead to her making other sounds that you can encourage. To teach her to *bark* on command, it is necessary that you use a stimulant that makes her *bark.* Try having an assistant knock on the front door or make a strange sound. Many times if you make a barking sound or walk around your neighborhood to find another barking dog, she'll be happy to join in. Try to duplicate situations that cause her to *bark* naturally, then praise her for it. If possible, stop her barking by gently holding her muzzle, but never actually squeeze it closed. Then give her the *bark* command as you release her muzzle to *bark* again. Reward her with a treat and repeat the exercise. You merely need to link her barking with the *bark* command.

Once your dog is talking on command, it is time to use it at the end of the *bow.* The plan is to have your dog talk to the crowd as she raises back up from the *bow* position. Wait until the *bow* training is well along and she is resting her muzzle on her paws before incorporating it. When she is consistently performing the *bow,* begin releasing her with the *okay* hand signal but require her to speak before rewarding her with the treat. The *okay* hand signal is done by turning both of your palms up and raising both hands skyward. Initially, use the *okay* command along with the hand signal so that she gets the idea. At first you can expect her to be standing before she makes the vocal sound. With practice, she'll vocalize as soon as possible so that she can get her reward. You won't even need to tell her to do the particular sound. Later you'll be able to drop the verbal command and signal her without your audience knowing.

Final Thoughts

It is important that you position yourself back toward the center of your audience so that it appears as if your dog is doing the *bow* to them. Also, if you plan on taking this trick on the road, practice it in various locations so that she'll get used to performing it in different situations.

Overall the *bow* is a classy way to accept the crowd's applause. It's a fitting end to a "command" performance!

When you have taught this trick, you will have a head start in teaching the tricks found in Chapters 2, 9, 10, 11, 13, 17, 19, 20, 22, and 24.

Marquise, an eight-year-old Samoyed, takes a bow, *ending her "command" performance.*

Other Useful Books

Alderton, David, *The Dog Care Manual,* Barron's Educational Series, Inc., Hauppauge, New York, 1986.

Antesberger, H., *The German Shepherd Dog,* Barron's Educational Series, Inc., Hauppauge, New York, 1985.

Atkinson, James, *Chow Chows,* Barron's Educational Series, Inc., Hauppauge, New York, 1988.

Baer, Ted, *Communicating with Your Dog,* Barron's Educational Series, Inc., Hauppauge, New York, 1989.

Fiedelmeier, Leni, *Dachshunds,* Barron's Educational Series, Inc., Hauppauge, New York, 1984.

Frye, Fredric L., *First Aid For Your Dog,* Barron's Educational Series, Inc., Hauppauge, New York, 1987.
———, *Mutts,* Barron's Educational Series, Inc., Hauppauge, New York, 1989.
———, *Schnauzers,* Barron's Educational Series, Inc., Hauppauge, New York, 1988.

Gudas, Raymond, *Doberman Pinschers,* Barron's Educational Series, Inc., Hauppauge, New York, 1987.

Kern, Kerry, *Labrador Retrievers,* Barron's Educational Series, Inc., Hauppauge, New York, 1987.
———, *Rottweilers,* Barron's Educational Series, Inc., Hauppauge, New York, 1991.
———, *Siberian Huskies,* Barron's Educational Series, Inc., Hauppauge, New York, 1990.
———, *The Terrier Handbook,* Barron's Educational Series, Inc., Hauppauge, New York, 1988.

Klever, Ulrich, *The Complete Book of Dog Care,* Barron's Educational Series, Inc., Hauppauge, New York, 1989.

Kraupa-Tuskany, H.F., *Boxers,* Barron's Educational Series, Inc., Hauppauge, New York, 1988.

Kriechbaumer, A., & Grünn, J., *Yorkshire Terriers,* Barron's Educational Series, Inc., Hauppauge, New York, 1990.

Lorenz, Konrad Z., *Man Meets Dog.* Penguin Books, London and New York, 1967.

Smythe, Reginald H., *The Mind of the Dog.* Thomas, Bannerstone House, London, 1961.

Sucher, Jamie J., *Golden Retrievers,* Barron's Educational Series, Inc., Hauppauge, New York, 1987.
_____, *Shih Tzus,* Barron's Educational Series, Inc., Hauppauge, New York, 1991.

Ullmann, H.J., *The Dog Handbook,* Barron's Educational Series, Inc., Hauppauge, New York, 1984.

_____, and E. Ullmann, *Poodles,* Barron's Educational Series, Hauppauge, New York, 1984.
_____, *Spaniels,* Barron's Educational Series, Inc., Hauppauge, New York, 1982.

Vriends-Parent, Lucia, *Beagles,* Barron's Educational Series, Inc., Hauppauge, New York, 1987.

Wehrman, Stephen, *Lhasa Apsos,* Barron's Educational Series, Inc., Hauppauge, New York, 1991.